Do Words Dream Themselves Into Silence Told In Riddles?

Do Words Dream Themselves Into Silence Told in Riddles?

For permissions and information on ordering books, contact operations@smallharborpublishing.com.

Cover art: Megan Merchant, "Do Words Dream Themselves Into Silence Told in Riddles"
Cover design: Diana Baltag
Interior design: Claire Eder
Publisher: Allison Blevins
Executive Editor: Kristiane Weeks-Rogers
Managing Editor: Bianca Dagostino

DO WORDS DREAM THEMSELVES INTO SILENCE TOLD IN RIDDLES?
SHANTA LEE HONEYCUTT
ISBN 978-1-957248-65-3
Harbor Editions,
an imprint of Small Harbor Publishing
Special thanks to: The Wild & Precious Life Series and Kristin Vandeventer

Do Words Dream Themselves Into Silence Told In Riddles?

Shanta Lee Honeycutt

Guest Featuring Goonphucker

Harbor Editions
Small Harbor Publishing

Thank you, thank you for hearing my voice
Thank you, thank you for making that choice
It's you, the reader, I dedicate this to
For now you are coming with me through and through

You'll hear this, you'll see that
You'll watch what you know on the page which seems flat
But it is deep and full, more than you know
For part of this is the Goonphucker show

Thank you reader, I dedicate to you
begin your journey, For at the end you are anew

P.S. Remember on your trip from here to-to
That I'll be there observing you

Contents

Do Words Dream Themselves Into Silence Told In Riddles?

"I'll never make it tonight. No trapeze on full moon nights.
Not the last time. I have to wake up from this dream.
The circus is over. All over."

—*Wings of Desire*

"We speak of time and mind, which do not easily yield to categories.
We separate past and future and find that time is an amalgam of both.
We separate good and evil and find that mind is an amalgam of both.
To understand, we must grasp the whole."

—Isaac Asimov

"You told me that our existence is all about choices. You said our choices create worlds. And so, theoretically, we simultaneously inhabited an infinite number of them. You told me that in this world, the worst choice you made is the one you made with me."

—*Dark Matter* (Television Series)

Rule 1: Everyone must play.
Rule 2: No outsiders allowed.
Rule 3. Nobody leaves.

—Rules from the movie *Braid*

"I think I should play the part until it's played out."

—*Persona*

Dark Things We Don't Know Much About

Prologue

& those two pistols embossed on skin in the back of knees that bend a lot & we know nothing about the way she changes her dress from red to black (or from black to red?) & the other one, the one who arrives well past last call, concrete kissed toes of the girl in the blue dress (can't be confused with the "Devil With The Blue Dress"). No one is sangin when this one wears it that way.

& Neo-Mary's in the parking lot in body con before we call these such things. Cord tied around her waist, the baby-that-isn't-Jesus in hand. Memba that otha woman? The one who says, *Remember when I said the gangs are chasing me…I lied. I'm Crazy.* Memba how the corners of mouth skin stretched between *I'm* and *Crazy,* trapping her ears against wide cheeks the way she trapped you in the bar's booth (be careful, she'll keep you there with her untruths). And we listen to the woman because her voice hitchhikes us over the Mason-Dixie and when we say Janis is reborn when you hear her saaaaaaaaaaaaaaaaang? We mean it. So stay in the bar's booth, risk the untruths. This one'll eventually have a song.

No song. She says the car, you know, the one Neo Mary's tethered to with the baby-that's-not-Jesus? It's hers.

We watch. We imagine they are cleaning it out.
But whose baby is that?

& it was always in a darkened part of the bar where seein learned me good. Eyes caught by the mid-drift, tight pants, and bad weave sitting on a bar stool with a 350 lb, 6'5 shadow of a man who refused to leave her side while she scrolls, holding up her phone for all intended audiences. I watch my friend watch the screen of the phone held by this drunk griot, *This is my other outfit.* It's a 21st century Duchamp whose descended staircase is titled, *Degradation of the Nude.* It was always the way hear'n learned me good as a man still tells this story to any who will listen,

My guardian angels?
They don't interrupt or intercept.
Instead, they say to each other,
'Ohhh, this shit's too good.

Imma let'em.

We talkin . . or souls or…

Instructions:

It's true.

Each book, each piece of prose, each poem…everything always teaches you how to read it.

Here are the rules for how to read me:

1. Believe what you see. Don't turn away. Don't question.

2. Go all in. No pause. No stop.

3. If you do break any of these rules:

    1. If you do question, only question what isn't on the page.
    2. If you turn away, do not turn the page.
    3. If you turn the page, we suggest…well…

4. If there is an invitation to an adventure, go.
5. If there are rules, follow them.

6. Don't lose your place, if you do:

start over from this page,
the instruction page.

One more thing:
Don't keep time

I.
ANACHRONISIACS

Goonphucker, Goonphucker,
up in a tree
Goonphucker, Goonphucker,
looking at me

Goonphucker, oh Goonphucker,
what do you see?
The Goonphucker sees
all that can be

Everything doesn't make it to swallow

Everything doesn't rise to chew

They taught me about here

'bout the ways some bodies require, demand to be sucked in

Taken . . . whole

Some bodies stay untasted,

unwafered

No body, no kill

No blood

Hallowed Hunted Body

Sucking whole bodies started with nuns,
ended with his body, began in a church
Her body, his body, that body turned the wafer I could never have
He made women writhe. He made foam surface from mouths,
us, his sea, he, our Poseidon with how chests heaved
higher than waves, how legs were never stilled
Then came time to take him, in mouths, the worthy mouths
That wafer, his body, that wine, turned them all vampiric
He IS our maker training tongues to hunger

Who has to give a fuck about original sin with *this*?

This is the garden where we learned how our mouth works
With eyes, with tongue, and through learning us good through ache
He whose body was wafer was my first *You can't have*
Mama never let 'em have my body on Sundays
as I remained on a hard pew. Maybe if I tasted him
like they do, drink his blood like they do, eyes wet
with want like they do, then I woulda known how the tongue
got wildly tamed. A wild thing tasting original hunger taught by pimps
Mama never gave 'em, but they still took, took my body whole

Trained in how to want to devour a man
Trained in how to want to become like him

A body, my body, the body   the wafer they crave
                                                            to put the fire out in their throats

When He Comes, Will You Be Ready?

No one had any answers.

If I stared up at my mother for too long, she had a ready pinch waiting for me. I was forced to watch the woman writhing, foaming, and speaking in a language I didn't understand. They call it speaking in tongues. In between the organ music, the woman writhing, and the voices whispering, *She was touched by the Holy Ghost,* they gave their affirmation. An approval of what we all were witnessing.

*

Little Lena – "little" for the way she was named after her Mama and seemed to be her Mama's twin – always had the answers, and this Holy Ghost was raised in conversation the following week. Something about the devil, hell, and how we all knew where we were going. It was one of those quiet and still summer days when the street and houses seemed empty because people were doing something more fun in another place not here. Here, we owned the street as we walked. Here, as we approached the house, Little Lena answered the question before I formed it. Silence smacked by her words, *One day, He is going to come. He is gonna to knock on every door. He is going to ask, 'Are you ready' You have to say yes.* She continued, *You have to be ready. Go with Him when he comes.*

I spent four years after that summer trying to figure out the *what* and the *He* who would be coming while trying to envision what this place looked like until we moved into *that* place—280 Collins Street. The lights are always a low hum of white fluorescent that washed over the cheap area carpet in the hallways. The hallway is long leading to a set of double-gray doors that, upon being opened, led to another long hallway with more apartments. And yet more around the corner just when you thought you had come to the end.

This…this would be the place where He would come knock on each metal, gray door and ask, *Are you ready?*

*

Sometimes, there are warm standstill summer days, like today, like the ones that Little Lena and I enjoyed. Forest Street is a quieter stretch before crossing Asylum Avenue. During this time of day, the St. Francis parking lot is abandoned. Few footsteps bounce off concrete, mostly my own feet as my mind conjures the unnamed woman writhing in church. This woman, touched by hands unseen, the Holy Ghost, and the shouting. I hear organ music along with Little Lena's explanation,

He is going to ask, 'Are you ready?' You have to say yes.

Everything is interrupted by a white van parked two feet away from this end of the St. Francis parking lot entrance. It's got no windows except the ones for a driver and a passenger. Right now, it's got no passenger, no driver. I move closer to the black iron gate that surrounds the St. Francis parking lot, almost bumping into a woman who stops me. *Hey baby, what's your name?* she asks in that familiar-older-Black-Woman's voice. Except she doesn't look like those words should pass through her lips. I watch the van. I pay attention to her.

She continues with her interrogation, *Do you live around here? Are you saved?*, and her mission, *Let me tell you about Jesus*…I am sandwiched between the curb, the white van, the black gate, and this woman's Jesus. I want to go home. They know what time school ends. There is no one walking down the street to see this. There are no cars casually passing down the street. So, no witnesses. She continues talking to me. She commands me to hold her hands. She tells me to close my eyes (she sees when I don't and immediately follows her instructions with a threat).

Her grip tightens as I feel bits of her saliva on my face, word fragments hit my ears...*don't want...oly Ghost...spank you.* Pressure around my fingers continue as air, words, and her saliva continue to hit my face.

I don't understand other things she says as she reminds me of that woman from that day in church, the one who's mouth foamed while she writhed. My body rocks gently, is it her? Is it my heart beating faster? I don't understand the van being so close, the street, the stillness...Little Lena's advice to *say yes* and *be ready.*

Is this woman the Holy Ghost?

I feel the circulation start to return to my fingers, the pressure from her grip loosens along with the words, this time with no saliva, *Have a blessed day.* The strange woman releases my hands and walks away with no warning. I am not sure how long we were standing like that but I can open my eyes now. I am two minutes away from home. I hope I don't get in trouble.

*

No one is home now. When did they leave? 280 Collins feels abandoned, with the exception of the knocking. It starts at Apartment 400. That knock is dressed in four steady paced thumps, unattached to any voice, firm enough to capture attention. The knocking continues at each apartment door until it is my turn.

Is this what Little Lena was talking about?

You can't report what's gone missing if you handed it over

The Corpsed Eater

They look like people. They sleep in beds
They sometimes . . . Corpsed eaters, Robber
Bridegrooms, a slick talked gang of thieves
with caves that are whole wombs, stomachs
cradling undigested rot   *want bloomed from
the tongue baby.* Severing, dismembering . . .
a subtle art. The best thief can snatch,
trespass with no protest. A Corpsed Eater
starts through the eyes, a slow, steady,
studied seduction maintained by how they
say how they've fed, how they've observed . . .
pieces go missing with touch, your tongue,
your language, gone with open space as the
caldron. Your body fit in the in-between space
of betwixt & exchange. *All exchange rates
have prices.* Imprinted scent. The butcher isn't
always the one who holds the cleaver.

Blame No One But (I)

penciled words imprint upon me, they all missed the faint marks dug into my skin from a madman, from the one who thought, *A rabbit, maybe 2 perhaps 3,* whatever will do for his wife's stew, his written thoughts *They. Made. Me.* i'll repeat what was wrought from a bound mind never freed *Rabbits for the stew i'll shoot three or few send the oldest for ammunition they tell me, they scream, they must meet today, the youngins go first their bodies will not quinch the thirst next the wife who suffered enough life barely back from recent birth they tell me, they scream,* RELIEVE HER OF THIS EARTH *next the oldest or save for last? she's the root of all this… this too shall pass, next is the boy then babe in its crib let it live? better dead? My end my life i'd care not to know, they'll say and keep saying it never mattered once i go* they'll write songs and tell tales and say no one knew but i do and i saw and so i'm tellin you I am the bow to a violin i strike sound before that i was sturdy and round held icing'd raisin cake bathed in festive sounds of Christmas Day i know i see i saw all whom sleep refused to wake i am a wooded womb of fetuses that are the sound and noise of a house that never rest i am the wooded womb carrying women gathered and their secrets and their tears and their words and their ask *what's next* i know i see i saw secrets imprinted upon their pupils like restless children refusing their beds

i can tell you how a family goes wrong
i can tell you how secrets seed the rot in a foundation
i know the white space between the letters
iknowiseeisawiknowseesawisawiseeiseeisee

Close your eyes. Breathe slow.
Hear it?

First, the female postmaster says

her mother tried to kill her
Met up with her in the ladies room, told her the details
of what she wished she did, her ma that is
She said, Ma said *I tried bleach, it burned my vocal cords*
She said, Ma said *I ate   and I ate   I swallowed*
I refuse, the postmaster exclaims, she said,
Ma said this and more with instructions,
Find him. Kill him. He started this. I was in the bathroom stall
the postmaster says. The postmaster says, *I'm ready.*

You call *Next, have your packages ready*
I'm next in line and I am ready. I steady my eyes
I take a close look, you refuse to know what you told me
Weeks ago? Months ago? Those dark circles ago?
Now a little faded. The fluorescents bounced off skin
the same way they did the night I thought, *She's got*
a rabbit's face (all humans look like some kind of animal)
It's you, I say, *we met,* I whisper, *what happened in the stalls?*
No met my ears from her gaze, *We've not*

Where are these going, she asks. She demands.
We play the same all do, dance with *I don't know you*
Spin with *I've never seen your face.* Go home with, *I want*
to forget. Where, you say. *Here,* I say. *How many days,* I demand
Your brown eyes, rabbitesque jowls, refuse me entry or exit
This part of our game moves in silence. This part, it ends.
Then, she's not a postmaster. There, she requests, *My sister,*
forgive her. Twins? I ask. Bad beer breath, tatoo'd bodies,
and noise discard my question

I went there, she said, *to kill my father,* jowls tightened
Eyes, steady. She makes me forget. She makes me question:
How far does the shadow of the asylum stretch, covering our bodies?

Tell me again
Show me the times,
the ways you catch me,

stuff me

Vanish air from my lungs

Over

and over

again

And again

Bring me to that place. Show me again
the cold pupils across space. How they
arrived to show me how the end feels.
How they are the last thing I see.

Bring me to that place

No hesitations
No questions
All gimme

Yours,
Not-Yet-Fevered-Feral

Instructions for unzipping the feral:

1. Start at the end; Or
2. Start from the beginning "Fevered Feral I"

But we dare you to do something dangerous. Start at the end.

Fevered Dreams of a Feral:
Where It Ends
Fevered Feral III

[Fevered Feral]

You may be wind, but I told you about the women from here

I come from distended belly extended
from breadcrumbs mistaken for full meal
how the sum of all them whispered home
I'm from the place of women who dwell
on the floor of fallen dry leaves. They are
the more than the sheets that never have
enough. How appetites stay growling
in eternal corpse pose. **We so used to**
dying here. Supple, falling, folding, wrinkling
Detaching with such grace it's what makes
them watch and say our drowning is
a thing of beauty. **We midwife each**
other through such thangs. Closed, open
private invitations with a quiet loud,
a shameless howl in wee hours through
day that ears refuse. The women here got
endless wombs, bottomless mouths,
unhomed. So hardened by the elements,
hands never appear, and for those that do,
their weight carried on the shoulders
of witness while our lungs and blood break
umbilical cords, bloodied hands bond in birthing
Brambles kiss feet. **We know each other in**
our naked as sisters by midday

And night? Reserved for the way we
became wedded . . . we, the unmothered
stayed naked and unspoused laying
with each other in the way we dared a
him to . . . You knew us by the weight of your
Can't . . . yet, you refused . . . Our sprawl &
our lifin' in your peripheral . . . you refused,
yet you felt us in the aborted unsaid, in
the kind of air that had no name that stuck
in lungs. **They clung to the other parts**
You knew us by how we cause the goose-
fleshed hair to stand. You knew us by how
we were the straight combs to all unnamed
feelings. I told, warned   screamed
about the women here . . .

We hold hands
to mouth to ears, cupped
whispering the tell that is the warn about
what happens to all brazen tries

Fever Dreams
Fevered Feral II
[Fevered Feral]
[Hunted Feral]

Haunchin' in the shadow of full white orb
His voice left echoes
that won't attach to the cave's wall

That time, I single Mama our children
That time, Desolation's colic won't end
I fed her parts of her papa,

like her papa, she won't quit
Scorch threatens to mark my body
as she did her father's body

The twins, No Named for
the way I killed him before
he named what we created

The baby I carry? She won't
mak'it till dawn. I dare her further
by refusin' to bury her placenta

My brood mimics my howl
I show them how to Night
teach 'em to get their own   not get got

Refusing all of me
They not gettin like Papa got . . .
Claws grow, lengthened proper

Tongue ready to lick meat off carcass
The papa of my brood blooms in the dirt
of Devil's Dew, he strengthens

He threatens he'll be back

We knew night
mapped toward
a low longing hum
an arrhythmia

Some say the________was what made the lips smack

Met him once
In a gas station once
The sock hop white R&B
The kinda slow played that way in that one movie

The one with all the cat people

We danced off beat
That voice made us end
rubbing the length and width of our trauma
self-soothing ended. Made him stand stiff

He's not moved since

This same night knew
I had no babies to feed Saturn to soothe his anger
My barren womb . . . I undressed every night
Let him take my flesh, my raw

My most difficult parts threatened to break his jaw

Saturn isn't the only one who eats bodies
Spent so much time in his belly, he taught me his way
Hot temper turned paternal,
loverly

Honey when you dine on bodies,
seek a man's heart, never his words
or his touch or else . . . you'll starve

We knew the thinning hours
The ambrosial hours we chased
when the wind was the fist
knocking the door open
When ears heard engines carry quiet and empty

Driverless

Within day being swallowed by asphyxiation
No shepherds here, but farm folk
A man aiming an indexed target at the sky,
explains to Son,

See the pale pink, how it swallows the
blue boy? It's an old one they say about
the Sun sayin he'd exchange his whole self
for a witness of her yawn Son

Pay attention

Only be that man to give that kinda love
Hear?

A girl, African Grandfather, and Jack Daniel's
are held between the index and thumb of thinning
and ambrosial hours where she tells him,
I am going to die doing this
There, African Grandfather says,

No. God doesn't work that way
You'll even be able to make
another and another and another trip
You'll die going to help children

His words wrapped like the coat she wears
and Echo being herself vibrates
in the bones of the girl

Die . . . like this . . .

Day heard the low hum felt
in the bones, an arrhythmia
I Corn Mama myself leaving tendons,
blood . . . my unsatisfaction in streets,
offices. Sometimes apartments,
sometimes bedsheets

The keep-keep on toil
and like all good work
this work has a song

Day's caught in the throat when Alice called
Dig that dirt from nails
bite 'em if we hafta
Spat out like chew of tobacco
    Nah, we don't spat
    We swallow the bits of glass
    the poison, the . . . all of it

We not your lusty thangs
We nobody's anything
We the hungry
The never fully fed
the . . . come Closer

In known dusk

The howl opens to the deep red,
back of the throat red

mouth, broken wide 'til teeth are on a flat plane

where a tongue remains
as wet as the engorged cunt
The one not contained in panties

She's the cave

Here I said
Now I said
Gonna swallow you, gulp you

Not said

Promised

You've neva' known a missin' like this
No gimme said
No yank felt. You won't feel gettin got
Imma take as I've always

But baby you'll. Be. Full.

In Mama Nyx's cervix
the drum spoke his voice
All things he hymned in silence
What he finna do when I said

I want it, like this

Once that howl was heard
of self, of vestments *no longer*
Now be you an imagined thing,
a figment of the untouchable thing

You be that very thing, in a box

In this cave lit where day's light can't touch
I am the horror, the hagged, the beauty
I've been had. I am the neva' touched
No idea have you that your mouth can't hold me

I am the unseen obscenity
I've murdered the toil in my bones
Let 'em starve in that field
Corn Mama's no more

I serve as I am served
I read his silences
He says his awakening, that utterance
is his is mines

In the dusk when moon dares daylight,

Take holla outta ya lungs
focus on where you grew me
Gonna bring you to where red disappears
The way earth is swallowed by water

I won't swallow you
Won't sacrifice my body to your yawn
Won't need pieces of you gone missin'

Imma need all of you for what we finna . . .

You've imagined none of this child

My body in his hush in the hum
of his desire, legs carry me to ambrosia
in the forever night tucked in my womb

My body broke day the way
my body won't succumb
to the low longing hum

How it grows
How it takes his voice
How it makes him have to use his hands

This Story Is About

A man on horseback
the way he is king
the way every clothed and unclothed
—babe, woman, man—is his

They told you this story
about the flow of the rivers
all the creatures, in wet, in sky,
on land and in the earth,
how the way the sun set and rose,
All this, he'd say, *is mines*

Including me

They told you this story
about this man on horseback,
how this is about him
about the hit of the hooves pon the earth
how another nameless beast
carries him to me

You hear about me after my throat is slit

You hear my bones, the way
they sang to the snapping
of the branches in the wind,
hear how my ears still straighten
to the vibrating ground,
my heart outpaces my legs as still as now's air

They describe how I sounded when I was caught

First taken up by the ankles
dangled upside down, my beast body
against another beast's body,
the paused wind and vibrating ears
all timing when my skin is parted from me

All are this story   caught   dead but

Dead is the only way he can see things

My round stilled darks
show him his reflection
How proud he is, his plans
for how he'll parade me,
wear my body, rest me
on his collar bone

His bones, the bones of his family . . .
nourished by me

This story is what imma tell
I'm the kill who caught the hunter
I'm the kill who eats, not swallowed
Dead, but not surrendered

Dead things, especially the thangs
of meat, of blood, of fur . . .

They have a way of corpsing the living

Haven't you heard about the rotting
that happens inside the stomach?

How a dead-live thang will eat yuh?
Make yuh a glutton from the inside out?

Sisters of She of Feral Souls, She Thangs, and…

"God's house is a simple house"

were the words presented on the building no different than the way words would often appear on tombstones that walk between worn and read. The day I encountered the structure, I almost missed it due to the overgrow. This convent was nothing like what I romanticized. The image of a grand building on the verge of royal, cradled by trees and hills. I never thought of seclusion serving a purpose other than space for silence. Devotion. Focus.

This was no royal leaning nor royal adjacent place. The bricks in disrepair were cradled by trees older than the name for my country of origin. The path that led to it wasn't much of a path. It was more like a simple manor in the forest. I had to promise not to disclose the "where" while disclosing what I do. I art. I tell. *For that*, they said, *You have to ask,* in a *this-is-not-to-be-mocked* firm tone.

Ask permission, they chastised.

Always, I said. Always because like any good breaker of boundaries, or trespass walker, you always ask. *Mother, May I….* I began. I never played the game as a child but I always knew that mothers were serious business. Here, at this obscure convent no longer, Mother is the one who came to be Mother Mia of the Sisters of She of Feral Souls, She Thangs and… Mmmmm

Even more serious? Minding the rule I always did in places like this. Leave whatever is found. And did leaving what is found include that which refuses to leave my thoughts? Did it mean or include leaving whatever finds you?

After the visit was arranged, I followed the instructions,

Mother Mia
May I?
Can I?

Legend goes she's the reason why some of us played this children's game (again, I never did). This is my first time sharing our conversations or more accurately, her words, and the words of those who followed in her steps channeled through me.

Before entering, do say the words of the Order of Mother Mia of the Sisters of She of Feral Souls, She Thangs and…Mmmmm

Mother. May I?

If you are reading this:

You are my children, sprung from my juices.
As my children, you are bound. You are binded.
In my image, you will remain.

Beyond words.
Beyond surface.
Beyond Chronos.

What binds you to me, binds to you, and
all that is with you.

Yours,
Spirit

(Letter 1)

Brother could no longer,
so I did God's work
History knows taking the prostitutes,
eventually, the single mothers,
eventually, their spawn, and their spawn
but history doesn't rhyme
It doesn't tell the truth
It is a jigsaw wrapped in riddle

I took her place
She taught me well
I vanished the clocks
I vanished the watches
Gone are the mirrors
Gone are the oil lamps

I vanished sleep
I vanished wake
This is God's work
Work requires devotion,
more than words
Elixir, more than sweat

The doing more than gesture
Floors require more than knees
Confessions more than an ass
sitting in claustrophobic booths
Do you really have something
worth being smothered for?

And each of you,
your lips, your tongues,
asked for healing, purification
But what will you pay?
What will you give?
Gods work? God's work is   starved

In some year of some Lord, they will say silence has a sound but we knew the flavors of such things. These such things accompanied by the kind of fabric that arranged the rest of itself on the body. Once past the head, once past the shoulders, the weight, tugs on the shoulders, to remind us, *We are the Sisters of the highest Order of Mother Mia, Keepers of Feraled Souls, the She Thangs. We are vessels of secrets, of their children, of each other, we are of*

this place.

The air did the rest of what this habit didn't, couldn't.

It's difficult only if you don't expect to pay.
It's impossible only if you don't believe.
There is one way to be that kind of faithful
Beholden

My child,

It is time and this is a truth. As I did not need yes nor tongue to see or say what must be done.

Surrender your sight so you can see.
Yield your flesh so you can speak truth.

For the rest of flesh knows the word. Knows the language.

Yours,
Spirit

(Letter 2)

Wound is a name attached to harm, scars imply
No name given to christen what's an omen. Faith
My plastered wrists, worn ankles, the way my feet kiss the floor.
Flat. One continuous shuffle, all earned by vows. The vows,

Teach me to embody and trust
All that which I will never touch
All that which I will never see
I am a mere and willing vessel
in his clutch

Humble me to give the holy floor
more than my knees
Never to earn glory
Never to earn knowledge or keys

Humble me

Take this one flesh
so my other flesh can speak
Take this vision
so I am rewarded the vision I seek
Let me ingest what is beyond sweet
I will swallow any and all to pay the debt.

Humble me.

Through these tunnels
Through our mattresses
Through the bodies
we know well, we know our way

When you find me and my sisters
with no eyes and void of flesh,
when you see me missing a tongue,
you need not be disturbed
You need not question

I am whole with the sum
of the most needed parts
I am pure with the sum of
no temptation

I am of God

They knew their
instructions

Find those who teetered
Seek those on the edge
of invisible. Bring them to
God's house, to She who
keeps them

It,
It instructed us
vows without question
the weight and air carried
upon our bodies with no objection
upon our conscience

The Takening happened
at the height of our cycles
It wrapped our hair in hand,
"Hoc es deorum opus" they'd say
or, *This is God's work with the*
holiest of offerings

Screams
Blood

Be the light before light is in the sky
Take mass. Be the minutes,
the hours, days with man's
makeshift telling

Rise is rise, rest comes with night
Be in thy habit adorned with thy chain
Adorned with thy leather strap
There is no weight when you walk with grace

Be thy face covered
As the veil exists
between and betwixt
A thin fabric upon your face, always affixed

You will be with child, his child
We will fill his lap, his house
With thy bounty
Give full body
Give full sight
Give and Give
Leave none for yourself child

You are ours are theirs

Child,

You are home and your body, our home
Whatever is living inside of you
Whatever rises up slow
Whatever inspires you to question child,
do you know what it is?

Are your ears trained to know?

Understand?

Yours,

(Last known correspondence)

The Albino,
he made me

Human chatterstry,
it ate me

The Gloomslinger's Riddle

I am of Mary's strong arms
for the way she'pound bread's dough
say they

Say they,
my eyes—not sockets—but twinkling blue
I'm lookin' right at you

See how full, how rosy they are?
I have Lisa's lips

And the thick, thick mane
of she who wouldn't shut it
If only, if only, maybe she could've kept it

From hip to knee, I was a waitress
My skin remembers their weary walking

From knee to ankle to left then
right mismatched foot,
you read adult, you read toddler,
skin of all in between

Feel all the ways they dangle
upon a book intended for prime
On the rope that announces the snap
Or even better… a bridge

Riding the rails and upon the tail of an Albino
From New Orleans to Pennsylvania
From New York to any
and no place

Unsettle your eyes
Undo the doubled take
See that I'm a childhood's sweetheart
See that I'm the almost in that one story
someone's children won't ever know

Taste the familiar name of that
one forgotten. Feel the gait you once
knew in that grocery store *or on the sidewalk, in the woods, in…*

Hear the way my hands are a familiar caress

I conjure smells of baked bread
The neighborhood that won't be the same
A scream that refuses to birth

the rest of me *Across the stomach of a field*
At the bottom of that one lake
An antithesis to the marked grave

I'm forever a specific turn of phrase
The tap of the middle finger's nail
crafted, sewn *of made companion*

I am made, I am stitched
with found remains, and sewn
Of open-eye'd nightmares I am,
I am imagination's children full grown

I be the lullaby
gripped by summer
I am the unheard wail
embraced by deep winter

I grow yet stay as I always was
crafted by a different wizard in this Oz
The Albino, they'll say,
they'll claim, he made me

They'll say, they'll claim
human chatterstry devoured me

,but bodies always tell when they think I don't see. My aim, precise. The boy with a body that fits into a mold of a man. A girl who means the face of a Mama who shouldn't know about bein sick and tired of the sick and tired **[few look at me the way she does. Straight. Unblinking. Certain all bad things are life are what happen just cuz.]** Far right, a wife too worn with the spark damn near jus bout gone, holdin the 7th one'a the youngins **[she tries to convince all is right, an almost unnoticeable upturn of lip, ever so slight]** One'a the youngins barely able to sit knows no better **[sheepish in front of my aim, he can't yet know shame]** One'a the youngins is right to look suspicious with slight side glance, the other youngin could care less **[he knows not about his papa's rot]** Nona these bodies scream in frona me **[Read.The.Eyes.]** Lookit Papa in the middle of all of it, trynna pull a wit on me and maybe the world he'll outwit. Papa's eyes can't do what the others can. His eyes, they hint a demise, of this whole affair, my eyes can't disguise his whole body with a slight chest poke outward. My eyes don't disguise how his whole body is bent to listen for instruction. It will read as if Papa holds the pose of proud. **Bodies always tell.**

Photo of the Lawson Family days before patricide on Christmas Day. December, 1929.

Blame No One But…(II)

of Pernambuco I'm not made,
but bow to a violin, I am
Before I struck sound
I existed sturdy, round
a fine one, they say

Blame no one but
the night before
penciled words
imprint upon me
they'll miss the madman's
marks, the one who thought of
a rabbit
or two
or three or few,
extra for his wife's stew

His writing
His thoughts
They invade me
I'm forced to repeat
what was wrought
from a bound mind
They tell me, they scream
A rabbit for the stew, I'll shoot
two or a few. Send the oldest
away to do his task. Today
will be the day. The yougin's,
they'll go first, will that
quinch the thirst? Next, my
wife who suffered enough
in this life. Barely back
from recent birth

Relieve her of this earth.
Next the oldest or save for
last? She's the root of
all this but this soon too shall
pass. Next the boy, next
the babe in crib…should I let it live?
My end, my life, I care not to know

I am but a bow to a
violin, I strike sound
before that, I was
steady and round

I held a raisin cake
I contained the festive
sounds of Christmas day
I knew the all sleep
refused to wake. I am
all the noise of a house
that never rests

I am the voices of the women
folk gathered. I stand the restless
children who refuse their beds
I am the vigil-keeper of all secrets
imprinted within their pupils

It ain't no trouble, but blood
causin' a coal shovel to
be used (enough to fill a wash
tub). Grass will never grow

from all them feet that had
to see. Raisins and bark
and a free for all for all the things,
now souvenirs from a crime's scene
for what they saw and can't unsee

and all ways that these things
are the best souvenirs for the
way they saw what happened

How does incest bloom?
Where does a family become undone?
Breathe. Slower. Listen.

In the old country with the last known one making his exit at the turn of the 20th century, there were Sin Eaters for the dead.

In some places, they sat with the body, they ate the bread that once rested on the dead. In other places, they did as priests do. For those whose lips remained frozen, they sat. They waited. This sitting and waiting, because doing the kind of wrong that felt good in life never suffered from being futile or fast. Never roamed the realm of *little* or *few*.

However, these stories forgot and forsake the Benefactrices of Pleasure, or simply put, Pleasure Eaters, who serve the no longer living.

Not necrophiliacs
No sex was involved
Not weirdos gone wild
They served a societal purpose, what do you think this is?
Not sirens of any rank or order
Not of the Holy, not quite
And no, not nuns
Not of the profane

Not. Quite.

So who were they?
What were they?

Like history and like the lists of deities only recognized for love, or lust, the Pleasure Eaters who expand beyond those cages are as unseen, erased. They are the deities who live in the interstitial space of the extremes of love, sex, and death.

Confessions of the Last Pleasure Benefactrix for the Dead:

The Last Pleasure Eater

It's time when the sweet ache begins
A tickle in the back of my throat,
a tingle in all tipped body parts, internal at first
A family member of the deceased summons me
My tasks simple, my preparations…detailed, involved
My gown with no fuss, no adornment with cloak
My face fully covered like my hair, like my skin

It's time when the sweet ache begins
The only flesh exposed and ready is my tongue
The space inside myself, prepared. Cleansed.
The white ash table furnished with body
within a room prepared for this meeting
The family has cleared space and path to leave me be
The air within this space also relieved of its duty

The time has come, my work has begun
My cleaned, days unfed tongue extends
Wherever is most needed is where I begin
A drag of my tongue along the neck's back
Linger behind the ears, savor what they didn't hear
Counter clockwise motions to return time to some parts
A pause, a break to consider
                                        the heart that can no longer quicken
                                        the loins that heat will no longer stricken

Time's come

Whispers?

My work is done

Words?

Ummm Mmmm
Ummm Mmmm
Ummm Mmmm Shhhhhhh

Take origi pleasure

union

Ms. Skein

What was of the light stays behind us. Bodies rise and fall, gently sway left and right in the dark. Sometimes the bodies, they move in the same direction as they are held by their thin barriers—glass and metal. A little cushion. Skin. The hard plastic sounds that refused to hold even itself.

The driveway is one of those clicheably long ones, where the dirt and small rocks demanded a price for being disturbed (a yanked undercarriage). They stop upon seeing the destination greeted by the warm light from one room and the figure that anyone can see as they approach the house. A figure who refuses to get up when one of the doors to her house is opened. The figure is a woman who is slightly larger than the child who accompanies the two adults. Her thick hair mimics a white pillow stuffed into a white pillow case when pulled back.

She does not smile.

Within the smile-less, warmless greeting, the child is pushed forward by the two women. The taller one has a nose that is slightly straight and slender body with a slight pretty face interrupted by heavy eyelids. Her hair, a small black halo of loose curls, adds to a whole look like one of those 1970's Black bodies with a fake smile convincing all onlookers that the Jheri Curl is a good thing. It is good for you. The woman with the Good-For-You-Jheri-Curl face and hair is in a crocheted vest with vertical chunky colored stripes against a heavy cream backdrop.

Good-For-You-Jheri-Curl is with a woman whose hair looks like autumn. The braids are straight down, what they call, "micro." This woman with autumn braids does not smile. She is shorter than her friend, yet, taller than the child. Autumn Haired Woman is dressed in a non-descript halter dress, a blouse (the Autumn Haired Woman never liked showing her arms), and simple sandals. The Good-For-You-Jheri-Curl Woman and the short Autumn Haired Woman know the woman whose face is framed by a puffed ball of white.

This is the woman's house.

The woman's face is framed by a puffed ball of white. She wears a face that sometimes appears as smooth as her formica counters to having features that rearrange themselves causing her face to squinch up like a prune. Ageless-Prune-Faced-Woman is known as Ms. Skein, like skein of yarn. Ms. Skein, never-married-no-children-no husband-miserly (that's what the adults praised her for, the miserly part). Ms. Skein doesn't say much. Ms. Skein let's the air say what she doesn't: *Ya'll the ones who came to see me. I didn't ask.* Her face punctuated by a turtleneck the color of the one room they were all allowed to stand in.

Like Autumn Haired Woman, the room is a deep pumpkin with warm undertones of reds, no bright colors. Just the warm ones, though the room and house feels as thick as the kind of old tree bark that can contain a certain kind of cold, like the cold within this house. The child knows that this is the kitchen because of the round table that this Ageless-Prune-Faced Woman sits at. Autumn Haired Woman and Good-For-You-Jheri Curl Woman stay standing. The child needs to use the bathroom. Ageless-Prune-Faced Woman speaks pointing a skinny, spidery, wrinkled finger towards a hallway that is pitch instead of lit.

There, child, at the end, she says.

The shadow of a wizened finger exaggerates the directions given by Ageless-Prune-Faced Woman, especially the words, *at the end.* Later, when the child grows into a woman, she will remember how Ageless-Prune-Faced Woman carries Black Widow spider well. The way she embodies spinning a web leaving just enough space to draw others in. The way Ageless Prune-Faced Woman only offered anything is through the instructions she gave about getting to the bathroom, but never offered a seat to sit, no food to eat, nothing to drink. The child now woman will reason that Ms. Skein did have a husband, or rather, husbands. None of them survived but she did. Alone. Within an ample house on ample land.

When Ms. Skein instructs the child about the bathroom, there is no difference between "in there" and outside. There is no difference between the voice within Ms. Skein's body and the slight cold of the air.

The child does not want to go to the bathroom but must.
It knows what happens to those who don't go.
The child begins the walk to the bathroom with Autumn Haired
Woman, Good-For-You-Jheri-Curl, and Ageless-Prune-Face
disappearing with each footfall.

The child walks with a rule bestowed upon her by Ageless-Prune-Face, held in tact by her loins:

And you bettah not flush the toilet. We don't do that here.

How to Be in Amish Country

It starts with looking for an Amish quilt, a belated house warming gift during a graduation. Journey away from the signs that promise "Amish Experience." Keep driving and worry about going in the wrong direction because the strip mall—it goes and goes and…watch the subtle change of the landscape.

A lush green field not left alone, attended to by a body using tools of the old country. Forget that you were worried. Forget that you don't realize that you no longer see restaurants, stores. Something is different.

A woman tends to her garden, the thick black fabric of her skirt daring to kiss the ground. She moves like its not 95 degrees with high humidity outside. The stops here are inevitable because an Amish quilt? It's one of a kind.

Small, folksy signs guide the stops and starts. The one house with the two women & three children. One tends the laundry and another waves one of you over while the other takes you and your friend into the modest garage with all the quilts.

Because options must be weighed, the drive continues. The heads of men sometimes covered in straw hats, sometimes covered by rounded brims of black, felt flat tops met with thick whiskers. Suspended chests held by black straps and white cotton.

It's the last house where the Dutch is thick, where what they have is the *more-than-quilts*. It's this home surrounded by summer heat that is thickened with the Pow-Wow and the car that brought you here is the only thing that announces the year. It's sometime in the 2020's.

Let your friend be the one to go carefully look at the quilts. You will look at other wares. Notice the tools that were being used to garden. Analog. Of this, a homestead is made. The furniture and heavy wood join in to speak of the way it's been here longer than the car parked outside. Longer than all of the lives contained within it were ever a mistake or life-planned thought.

The wood floors absent of creaking chime in. They put you in your place to remind you that they were here longer than your birth, your Mama's birth, and your Mama's Mama's birth. They give permission to the walls and handmade everything to tell you to shut up about hunger. They whisper, *None of it feeds you like this.*

If the fridge dared to hum, it was low. No buzz of modernity causing ears to ring. But don't just take the quilt. Take the pieces of the dialect you don't understand within questions, *How does that hold against the not-so-far out there?*

Your body will long to feel the weight of that fabric hanging off your body with a bonnet in the 95-degree, high humidity weather. The tongue wonders if it too can bend to the dialect not passed and passed and passed.

A hand vibrates under a steering wheel that vibrates from the tires meeting the ground that stretches towards the nearest strip mall. A finger twitches wishing it snapped the old man leaning against his garage, pipe in hand, and unapologetic stare steadied under that rounded, felt flat hat.

His body framed by white barn doors with a wagon just beyond. And the things only caught by the shutter that has no button or ready replay. It's here at this stoplight just ahead you replay the way a shadow dodged the sunlight lighting the kitchen floor in the last house.

In the last house, a pair of feet from the outside stayed in place *What were you staring at? Why were you so still?* Edges of a black, felt, flat brim, no whiskers yet, but black suspenders against white cotton holding adolescent curiosity caught within the eye of the outside world.

And yet, no hairs announced that you were being watched. *Is this what calm does?* It was here in the valley of the growing strip mall—a sadness that a certain truth is remembered:

Some images were never meant to be captured.

& the trespassed spaces within the Ephrata Cloister
& the wooden blocks they used in place of pillows
& the saliva that grows on my tongue

Could I

Could I

The Goonphucker is on a branch and sees all in a trance

When you meet the goon or the phucker or both in the tree
What you will say is *Who is me?*

Who is me? As I pep the pipe
The Goonphucker knows what's left and ripe

The Goonphucker sees, the Goonphucker sees

Beyond the tree

THE ABRIDGED INDEX OF PLACE

By M.M. Jones

Contents

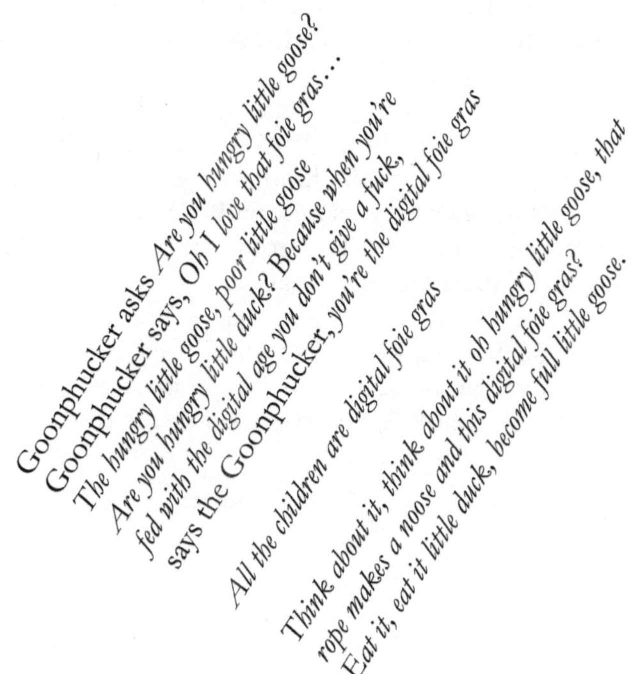

Goonphucker asks *Are you hungry little goose?*
Goonphucker says, *Oh I love that foie gras…*
The hungry little goose, poor little goose
Are you hungry little duck? Because when you're
fed with the digital age you don't give a fuck,
says the Goonphucker, *you're the digital foie gras*

All the children are digital foie gras

Think about it, think about it oh hungry little goose, that
rope makes a noose and this digital foie gras?
Eat it, eat it little duck, become full little goose.

It was one of those fancy places

They called it a tea room…fancy heavy drapes just beyond the door. One of those fancy places cradling mystery with a slow undress to reveal what you are about to enter. It's where you can't know yet what you can't know what awaits beyond the heavy curtains.
Prepare for what awaits by pulling the curtain back.

Off to the left, you see teeth accompanied with a slightly pointed nose belonging to a voice attached to a grin. You catch a flash of something red. Something dangling. You enter beyond the curtain. You look at the case. You look at the menu. Funny. You don't see anything red.
No red velvet. No beets. Nothing serving that kind of stain or flesh.

You steal glances while placing your order. Your eyes are drawn to want…more red stains. Something in the way she opens her mouth. Something in how her face paired with her hair with the pointed nose and how none of it matches. You go to the restroom and you return.
Take your hot chocolate, it is ready.

She is no longer talking, the red stains draped by her lips, eyes stare into the screen of her phone. You stare at the floor as you leave, slowing the pace of your walk. **Look for the red. Look for the flesh.**

You are hungry.

Memory Works Like Jumping from Julian to Gregorian: What About That Manor?

The story goes that when there was a transition
from the Julian to the Gregorian calendar, some
went to bed on February 21 and awoke March 1.
In 1582, Pope Gregory decided to end the day,
October 4, and skip to October 15. And he had
to change things, otherwise, every 314 years
would add an extra days, extra days add up.

Some places took longer.
Some places killed more days.

Memory works like jumping from Julian to Gregorian. One day is as it presents itself, the next is based on what is remembered or said, or touched. *That's it too,* they said, *the more you touch it, the more it changes.*

M e m o r y

Why did it have to change each time we touched it? Looked at it?

The house is not what I would call simple. Two stories high, marble. And imagine entering an open space that's just white with some color? Enough color as not to cause visitors to be caught off guard. Almost like they wanted the place to look like some kind of normal. The first thing they wanted us to know is that they did not rent to Indians, I found that odd given that the gentleman, the one describing the place, he was Indian.

*

The manor is not what I would describe as simple. Rishi, the owner of the property apologized, *Sorry, we have no rooms available.* We'd just gotten off a 12-hour train. *The fog, ohhhh, the fog, it is always like this*, they all said. Even Rishi. But not wanting to turn us away, he says, *I have a place.* His skin and teeth seemed uncomfortable with the stretch of his smile when he said, *plaaaaaaaacccccccccccce.*

The place was located in the back. Hidden by the stairs, trees, and the fact that it sunk into the landscape like it was hiding. Two stories high. No columns (because one would expect columns on a place like this).

Rishi jiggled one key, two key, a third, then a fourth, finally opening the door. I want you to imagine entering the foyer of a home that is white with marble with touches of color. You know the kind of color…a bit of black and white tile here, a purple door there, an odd yellow over yonder (was there any yellow?). Enough splash to say to any visitor, *This place is normal. It feels normal. See!* I forgot to tell you, one of the first things about this place Rishi says is this, *No Indians.* His uncomfortable skin, teeth, and smile become the backdrop of all of this while his eyes are fully charmed by his own statement.

He saw confusion.
He heard my uncomfortable laugh.
He continued as if encouraged, *They are dirty. They steal.*
How funny. I thought he was the *They* he was talking about.

*

That manor is one you might call both simple and not.

You arrive after a 14-hour train ride. You came back from Varanasi, known as the land of the thin veil with cremation grounds along the ghats. You are so tired you forget that you were told, *Sorry, no more rooms,* and this is a big deal because of the two major hills to climb to get to this tourist complex. The first one is guarded by a leash-less, happy Great Dane named Pearl. She's happy and though you know this now, your heart stopped the first time Pearl came out of the gates, running down the hill of the house on this hill to greet you. After your first meeting with Pearl on this first steep hill, you became so curious about this house on the incline.

You get to the second hill and meet a guy. You forget his name and when apologizing about your middle of the night arrival, he says, *It's the fog this time of year. The deities dictate the time, we are just here.* You notice the way his smile widens when you ask for a place, *We are all booked up but I have a place for you.* And when you retell the story, you'll talk about the details of him including someone else as if you are not travelling alone. You will always feel like someone else got the story wrong but never you. You remember this detail of a so-called nother because he is making eye contact with the other traveler. *Who is the other traveler? Can fog induce PTS, Phantom Traveler Synbdrome?*

But that isn't the important part, it is how he then says, I *don't rent this place to Indians.* It's how the tone shifts from jovial to telling a secret, yet, still maintaining a volume like he could care less about who hears what he is saying.

You follow him and you notice you both move away from the congested, tourists-with-rooms area to another place. You count these two steps, then four, then another set of steps. As you climb the next sets of steps, you notice two hills.

You and I-Don't-Rent-To-Indians, leave the light pollution of the short street lamps that lit the area of the tourist packed rooms and you move towards less light, less people, open sky. More stars.

You recall that you hadn't really noticed the stars in the three months you've been in India.
You play off giving the burn in your legs a break.
You play off stopping to catch your breath.
You notice that he is still talking about why he doesn't rent to Indians, *They are dirty*, he says, *Nasty*.
You wonder to yourself, *what does this even mean?*
You are relieved that it seems like every culture seemed to bash each other. *All humans are horrible* scrolls on an endless loop in your brain as you follow this dude.

You are not relieved when you see the place. The place is located not just in the back, it seems to sink into the ground despite all of the stairs you just climbed. You are unnerved. The place is secluded. Of all of the keys on his crowded key chain, you marvel because he finds the exact key to this manor.

You notice the 6 columns that seem out of place on the manor (odd, it seems like it shouldn't have columns). You notice that they are as white as the foyer. All white and marble except the odd floors that remind you of piano keys because of the black tiles against the white. You are shown to your room, but something is off. The way there are splashes of color with the white is unsettling. You also wonder,

Where is everyone else?

*

That place, it is not simple. It is not forgettable.
However, it is one of those places that if you leave any details out,
I mean any detail, the place itself will change or start to disappear.

That ever happened to you?

It happens in stories all the time. Move something from there to here.
Move something here, or erase it, and the story…it changes.
Look it up, they say this is true of human memory

That won't happen. I remember every detail.

The 100 lb. adult Great Dane named Pearl first appears menacing when you first meet her. That's the first major hill because the rest of this walk is a steady incline. The row of small apartments that are meant for the tourists. Two toned with the top part being the windows, framed in white paint and the bottom, some kind of red.

The manager's office across from those places.
The patio area. The same place where I got dangerously close to a King Cobra *the photos were worth it.*

That was all the first time I was there.

The second time I returned…well…this place because I'd acquired books and my Sitar, they were generous enough to hold it all for a small fee. So, you could say, I *had* to return. They had my stuff.

This time, a guy I'd never seen, I mean never in all my full-four-weeks-I-stayed here-before-kind-of-never, was in that office. It was evening due to the 16-hour train ride from Varanasi. It was fog season and it meant slower trains *I should've stayed longer. A week in Varanasi doesn't cut it.*

This guy comes out and shares, *There are no more rooms available but I have a place.* The way he says *I* didn't give it away. Not even the way he says, *I don't rent this place to Indians.* And not the way he continues, *I don't trust them, they are*…I can't remember what the rest of the tirade was because we were now climbing stairs. I started to count the stairs. 32 going up.

I noticed the way the stairs felt like another hill, or I should say two hills like the first hill I call Pearl's hill, *the Great Dane who greets all.*
I noticed that instead of a light that shines on all of the main courtyard in the main area with all the tourist rooms, light became a rare feature on this short trek. One light, maybe two on the wall that I never noticed, a wall that grows taller. A wall that seems older than any other place on the property and that was the thing. *Didn't this place describe the dwelling as compact? As the place where you meet this person or that person from other countries?* None of the trip guides mentioned anything about another dwelling on the property. It was best described as apartment living for tourists. What was *this* place?

The distance between each step was short and quick, yet, it made our trek longer. How long had we been walking for? That question became, *why was this man talking incessantly?* Then another why. Why was he so sure, so intent that I would say *yes* to this place?

Expecting pavement, it was now grass.
Expecting a straighter path, no incline, I almost tripped.
We dipped a little and I noticed the place.

The endlessly jaw-clopping man has a key ready approaching the door.

It's too late to say no.

*

An unsimple, unforgettable manor forcing the eye to take in its architecture. The windows. The door. The way that it should have had columns, but somehow, didn't. I realized that I remembered this place when I stayed in the tourist compound, there was one lone building that was in the back. Isolated.

The guy I never saw before had only one key in his pocket, the one key to unlock the white door. Strange, if you manage a place, doesn't that have a mandate of carrying many keys?

My pack was heavy. I entered this manor feeling like something was wrong and something was right at the same time. The tile was mostly white except the interruption of black reminding me of the last scene in Hitchcock's *Notorious*. All the doors in the place were closed. It was two floors in height with a slightly curved elegant staircase leading to the second floor. The guy tells me to take the stairs and my room is the one on the right. It is assumed that I will take the first room on the right, but there was no confusion because it was the only door on the right side. That was the other oddity. The positioning of the doors. The architecture was *off*.

The whole place was right and off at the same time. A vase here and there, sometimes a chair, sometimes a book, or some other thing to perform normal. How does a place perform normal? Splashes of color, and the right adjustment of this and that as not to sound any alarms within any human within its space. It is enough normal to be accepted. Enough that a place can appear as if it embraces the human form.

I noticed as we approached the entrance of the manor, silence took the place of his talking as if he was instructed or bent to heel to the silence.

I noticed that his smile was strained as his lips became slack from showing all of the teeth that he'd shown before as we approached this manor.

He never followed me inside past a certain point.
He explains my room, which one, a very specific one, though the rest of the rooms are empty.
He says good night robotically. He closes the door and leaves me alone.

Here.

I want to jiggle the door handles.
I want to yell *hello.*
I enter my room.
I am shocked by the Smurf blue and white palette.

It feels as strange as the occasional blues, yellows and purples in the otherwise white place outside of this room. I am refused all sound, even my own breath. Were all human bodies forced to succumb when entering this place?

I surrendered, but not to sleep.

"Signs will appear to men."

A part of a full sentence within an alleged letter Grigori Rasputin wrote to his daughter about his and his country's doom.

LET REASON

1. human balance
2. fitness diversity.
3. a new language.
4. passion—faith—tradition— all things wit reason.
5. people and nations
6. dispute in a world court.
7. Avoid laws and officials.
8. personal right with social duti
9. Prize the infinite.
10. a cancer on the Earth—Leave — Leave

GU ES S A REASON

1. Ma n 500,000,000 in nature.
2. r ise— and diver t
3. e a t language.
4. —faith— and
5. people and law and
6. nation rule e ternal
7. Avoid petty and useless
8. B e right with social duti
9. h— ea t seek the infinite.
10. Be not Leave room Leave room

GUIDES TO AN AGE

1. Leave room for nature
2. Maintain under 500,000,000
3. reproduc wisely—
4. Unite a language.
5. Rule with temper
6. Protect
7. world court.
8. Avoid laws officials.
9. rights with social duties.
10. seek harmony infinite.

Be not a cancer on the Earth—Leave room

Leave room

Nature

Seeds of Arson

1. Maintain humanity under 500,000,000 in
nature.
2.
3. Unite
4. passion—faith—tradition—and
reason.
5.
6. rule internally
7. Avoid laws and useless officials.
8. Balance
9. Prize truth—beauty—love—seek
infinite.
10. nature—

LET THESE BE GUIDESTONES TO AN AGE OF REASON*
(In their original form)

1. Maintain humanity under 500,000,000 in perpetual balance with nature.
2. Guide reproduction wisely—improving fitness and diversity.
3. Unite humanity with a living new language.
4. Rule passion—faith—tradition—and all things with tempered reason.
5. Protect people and nations with fair laws and just courts.
6. Let all nations rule internally resolving external disputes in a world court.
7. Avoid petty laws and useless officials.
8. Balance personal rights with social duties.
9. Prize truth—beauty—love—seeking harmony with the infinite.
10. Be not a cancer on the Earth—Leave room for nature—Leave room for nature.

*The Georgia Guidestones were built in 1980 and destroyed in 2022. Their reason for being and the "who" and the "what" behind them has remained part mystery and part conspiracy theory for many years. The case was possibly cracked in 2025 linked to a man who says he was concerned about the world's growing population.

Don't Blink: Curse of the Relief Who Hides in Plain Sight

Chapter 1: A postcard-come-to-life-once-a-movie's-set-partially-abandoned-town,

dead bodies, a mountain top, a day's journey, and a goal to break the law this time. A return, to the dead bodies and the crumbling structures. A return to break the law with video and photo capture.

Jail might be a thing if you get caught. Getting caught is a real thing because the tour group will descend the stairs to catch you because your dream said so. Being caught is karma, but this isn't. It and the crime is bigger.

Chapter 2: Don't move,

don't blink. Look. At. Me. Tell me if or what I am, do you understand? Tell me if or what I am what you see. Swallow me, my faceless stature, take me in, a hooded sight, my finger raised to signal, *shhhhh, I'm your curiosity's delight.*

A raised relief they declare. History of this place they'll claim.

Nay.

I'm none of these.

Chapter 3: It'll work as if made off with a secret.

I descend the stairs to leave, this high wall from another time — its height, its stature — my relief. No need for regret, no need to consider the exchange for this hard trespass. I've abandoned all guilt. The day is perfect for this crime and time is as hushed as the weather.

A surprise kindness for a criminal.

Retracing my steps as if this is familiar to my spirit, my body. In an hour's time, on a bus I'll be, leaving this postcard behind.
A mischievous soul at peace.

Chapter 4: At peace, you won't be.

A price must be paid, an exchange there must be for thinking you were free. For all who see me, touch me once is what you can't help. Touch me twice, drag your hand slowly. Trace my image. Now, you've ingested me. From my grip, from my hold, you'll never flee. Try me, push me out, same as they tried and tried and tried in the old country.

Take another so-called last look. Don't blink. You're taking me back to where you're from, my hooded sight, my finger raised to faceless lips, it tells you this time *Don't Protest.* I do not wash away with time.

I'll let you tell of your crime.
I'll let you speak,
I'll let you say, *I must confess*
as you stitch stories.

But of me, of this place, you will obsess because a confession is no fair fare paid.

For the exchange of doing what you shouldn't've did, I'll keep you. I'll stay with you. Of me, of this place, you will never be through. I will add you to all of my others who did what you dared do.

And tell all you know. Brag to your friends, perhaps your kin that you got away with it and that you might do it again.

Tell them all where you've been, repeat the theft woven in words over and over again,

Portali tutti a ME

Place: The Abridged Index

1A

Places are pain fields
Places are hurting fields

Or is it people hurt people, and the residue of these actions seeped into a place?

This was the first place to teach me how columns do not always belong. The place where the Greek Revival died in the execution of an idea. Too narrow to be called columns. Too narrow for bodies to try to fit, pass through.

I know it because of how I kept driving the same route. First the GPS showed me, now it stuck as the way to know this place. This place doesn't whisper but calls.

I go past and the next and the next…this time, I slow down to count how many

One

Two

Three

*Fo…*too many. *Don't they mimic bars to a cell?*

They are the bars to a cell.

Then there were those windows. You know, the kind that were *that* kind of old. So old that you know that they've not changed in the past 150 years, maybe longer?

I keep hoping that I knew exactly what to do to turn left, turn right, then go past this house.

This house, because it knows things.

2A

Places call us back
Places pull us in

It's the same building on the surface only to the eye that sees what it wants to see. Nondescript. A light brick. No windows. And to my eyes, there's something about where it sat at the crossroads. *I refuse ignoring,* it says, *My full one story-self won't be unseen.*

My breath, my body can't be easy in the presence of this building.

I always want to stop but as I slow down the building instructs, *Keep. Moving.* It's instructions reminds me of something a wise She said when presenting a question,

Don't you think that in New England, the roots of evil might be that of the religious kind, like the devil or something supernatural? And in the south, the evil is within the hands of man?

But what about the places not north not south, where evil is maybe manmade and maybe not a crafted supernatural happening over and over and over again in the shape of place?

3A

Places leave breadcrumbs out of sequence and hidden in the body

It wasn't until several years later that I discover that my paternal great grandmother, Betsy, a mixed woman who is Cherokee and White, is possibly from somewhere in Colorado. Finding her and her white father, great great gran, create more questions than answers. Family genealogy is like a case of lost treasure, like in the case of the Lost Dutchman's gold mine in the Superstition Mountains in Arizona. One might feel better about finding it.

Then again, would it be worth risking one's life for that kind of treasure?

A genealogical treasure hunt was not my reason for being in Denver and hunting for what I sought risked time. Being late to our destination. We didn't have long after our arrival to the Denver International Airport, before we had to jump into a cab, check into our hotel, and meet our clients.

I'm not sure I would have ever chosen Denver to vacation. Before this, I passed through it once. Yet, I always knew that if I ever encountered Denver again, I would need to see the airport. I would need to find *it.*

4A

Places are unrequited
Places will break parts of you
only for you to want to break the barriers to re- enter them

Be. Careful. These are the best and most horrendous ones

We crept across state lines into the Carolinas. Cicadas, night, and a different kind of gothic invaded our bodies. Some skin can shapeshift, eat night, kin with night sky and give you half a chance in a certain kind of place. Pitch painted bodies.

Especially the places that invite you to want in.

I needed to take a chance to go to Magnolia Boone Hall within minutes of crossing the state line. I wondered if I'd be able to see the silhouette of the canopy of trees the way I always pictured the stories about plantations that created a whole mythology about how history and place entangled.

Why and how does nature retain its beauty in the center of tragedy?

We go there, and I didn't expect the gate.
We go there, and I don't know better than
to stand at the gate.
A threat of a violation to get in.

I didn't know better than to wrap my hands around the bars, flesh pressed against black iron to see what I could read of the landscape as my eyes adjusted to the dark.

The cold metal and discomfort, causing my flesh to numb the more I pressed. And the way I did none of these things, but played this happening on repeat.

I drove away sad, but with a lingering question,

Why was I so hungry to run up to the gates of a plantation?

5A

Places train us up, mold us
Train our bodies how to move within them

Ever notice the way a place might inspire you to move ever so slowly, or perhaps a place dictates that you need to move at a pace you may not be aware of in the way that your body is being compelled within that space?

Ever think about how someone sets up a house in a way that dictates how bodies move within it?

For example, have you ever been in a home and noticed that there are cleaning implements within every room to imply that constant maintenance is needed, and therefore, one must stay vigilant about needing to maintain an all-white place as it is?

*

Growing up, there was a vogue for certain families to keep their formal living room encased in plastic. The main couch, the love seat, everything forever wrapped in ways that imply that if anyone were going to sit upon those couches, there would need to be a barrier between body and fabric. If anyone dared sit, it would be the human body, not the couch, that would be uncomfortable. The human skin would become stressed against the thick, hardened plastic covering the couch.

I never sat in one of those formal living rooms because it was never allowed. We only passed through the room or paused to notice how things stayed untouched and in perfect condition. I now wonder: did plastic encased furniture also create a barrier between and among those who inhabited these spaces?

My childhood is also filled with snapshots of the way that some apartments and homes had dining room tables arranged with permanent place settings complete with the thick plastic place mats and napkins and silverware arranged. Sometimes glasses. Sometimes plates. All set up in a way as if one were entering a restaurant.

When they ate, did they ever eat at these permanent place settings?

If places potentially mold our bodies in terms of how we move within them, how do we create place in ways that add to the creation, hardening, or softening of the mold? What other baggage do we bring to places we inhabit?

What do we leave behind that adds to the mold that lingers?

Places that eat ashes and bodies also eat other things
Places that eat ashes and bodies…they are never full

This place painted our bodies in that pitch as preparation
to meet the gods. Night needed to eat day. A ride arrives and
takes us through the narrow alleyways.
(Wait and wait…arriving at night is required)

Arrive to where you thought the place was all along. Beyond the congestion of bodies, but to the maze of alleyways that hover at your back and the steps that descend beyond where light travels.

Don't check into the hotel, at least, not yet.

Let a sari'd figure call to you from the dark. Let a stranger approach and your ears will resist him for the way your body wants the steps.
(Wait and wait and wait…the talking stranger is required)

Wait for the stranger to finish. Your partner turns to you and suggests, *"Let's climb down as far as we can. Let's see if night disappears the steps."* You notice the way the light bathes everything and everyone at the top of the steps but refuses anything past the 4th step.

Towards pitch.

Let your feet get accustomed to steps that existed before you and before your country. Sit on the steps. Dare the pitch to vanish you.

The eyes never get accustomed to this kind of dark. Ears never get accustomed to the…screaming? Howling? The body never adjusts to this kind of darkness. Be busy having a conversation about this womb while daring it to eat you whole. Be egotistical enough, self-centered enough to believe that the place co-created you (though, you were never in its consciousness.)

Have enough myopia to think that a whole country, civilization and all of its gods were inside of you, inside of your mother's womb, your grandmother's womb, and the whole line of ancestors.

You couldn't possibly think that you were important enough to be the tectonic membrane, the consciously conceived burp that arrived into all of this?

5B

Places train us up as bodies are molded and moved in the image of space

What are the rules of place?

Consider: Museums.
Consider: Walking into a friend's house with your shoes still on and discovering that everyone has taken their shoes off.
Consider: The shop that requires an appointment because of all the expensive items inside.

Consider: the way one's spine may stiffen in these various instances.

You are always on *their* terms. You will police yourself on behalf of space and place.

Then there are the places where you know you can't stay for too long because…rules that dictate.

Consider: The Sistine Chapel and Vatican City. No lingering lest you become separated from the group. You are in a group because this is the only efficient way to see it.

No standing to look at any of the 1000s and 1000s of pieces of art on the left and right sides that one passes at a high-speed while being led to the main jewel, the Sistine Chapel. *Remember the rule: Look. Up.*

Stay stuck with gaze…up

Once inside, you're allowed 10 minutes of standing with other bodies. Enough time to debate how long you will look right, look left or look up, given that you could look in any of these directions for far longer than the 10 minutes they give you. All of this doesn't give enough time to swallow this reality: The Vatican is its own entity?

Why is its own country, governed by the absolute monarchy of the Holy, a country ranked among the smallest in the world, given that it is less than point 20 square miles?

These are things you must find out after — after the visit. But the *while* part, the *during* part, you must try to take the whole in.

*

The why, how, when, and sometimes, who, of a place lingers long after. You think about the "before" after visiting. After venturing to Europe, India, the Denver International Airport, the landscape of the American South.

Places that no longer are and aren't are their own kind of alchemy. They have their own rules that dictate how you move within them and whether or not you can approach them. Sprawls of places that are as remembered and forgotten as most humans. What is forgotten stays forgotten until Costco. Until the condos. Until a hotel, or some combination therein is built on top of an asylum.

What is forgotten must stay that way because the signs and warnings of arrest will it to be so.

What are the rules for moving within a given place? *And what about the land?*

How does the structure invite or deter us from being there?
Is being deterred really an invitation to trespass? *And...land, the soil?*

The complexity of history. The ebb and flow of the human bodies in and out of a place, the coming and going across soil.

What about the places that hover between?

Consider: Nantucket

One goes to that island and wonders who lives on Nantucket versus working there versus who lives in all of the empty places? The abandoned places are the second or third homes during the *off* seasons.

But off-season has a charm. See the cobblestone streets for the first time. See a few of the quaint downtown shops. Drool over the pre-war buildings. Ask questions about the abandoned summer homes that are not charming but bearing icicles that will pierce the skull of anyone who happens to be walking by. Ask questions about the bodies being ferried back and forth because if you are really fortunate, you don't ferry forth and back. You go. You Stay. You leave only to return during *the season.* This for nothing less than the price tag of $9 million, depending on what year you see the house listings.

If you want to know a place,
ask the taxi cab drivers
the book store owners,

their blood runs the place
12th generation whaling
She's now driving a cab and looking for a place to live

And this place really comes alive in the summer when all of the
blondes descend upon the place
They have come to order their taxi rides
Their food
They own the streets
They reclaim their abandoned 3rd homes

If you are really paying and playing attention, a place will teach you like Nantucket teaches you.

Some places are not abandoned, they are just extra. Like having an extra pencil.

Just like places mold us, what if you are place—less then,

You are trained in pretending like you have a place.
You show up to school, you do the work.
You show up to work, you do the work.

Like everyone, you have a place unless:

A. You live in a hotel like those people on those soap operas (but what about the hotel hoppers? The people without the posh?). No, we're not talking about Howard Johnson or Hotel 6. Those don't come with room service. *But if you live in a hotel like the soap opera people, then…*

B. Travel or move around for work or during childhood (out of your control, but sometimes, you get the status of army brat).

C. A shelter, but that is something you can't…won't admit to. That does not count as *your place.*

There is always the assumption of place. The assumption of bodies in a place, living, breathing, being.

However, the rule is this: A place can be without bodies. We call that for sale or abandoned.

But bodies without a place?

4B

Places are unrequited:

You are always the one seeking out.
Be. Careful.

You were seeking it and therefore it is seeking you. *You wish.*

When we first arrived, I hadn't seen the blazing yellow eyed, blue bodied, 32-foot-tall fiberglass Mustang, Blucifer, outside of the Denver, CO airport until we were leaving for a flight out of Colorado. As the taxi wound its way to drop us, Blucifer was taunting me. How did I not know about him? And how did I not know he killed his creator by falling on him?

The random, quick sighting of Blucifer was a warning as I stared at this giant blue wonder until I could no longer twist my neck and body to see him. The "Children of the World Dream of Peace," is a different story.

I knew what I was looking for there.

And if you know what you're looking for in a place, will you feel better once you find it?

If you're drawn to a place, does it mean that somehow, that said place is in your DNA?

3B

Places leave breadcrumbs
Places tell you to pay attention

Things are easier to spot through a screen, blown up and out of context. Out of the context of specific location or discussion about where exactly.

How was I going to find these murals within a few minutes after arrival, within this 1.5 million square foot complex?

Like anything else, look without looking. Desire what you want to see while minding your business, say, going to look for the bathroom. While looking for the restroom, bump into, say, Leo Tanguma's "Children of the World Dream of Peace."

The image on the left is a scene of children rejoicing over a defeated and crumpled figure on the ground. The figure on the ground is in a WWII era gas mask, and he is not only defeated, but so is his machine gun as a rainbow of red, orange, yellow, green, blue and purple wraps as an arch over the whole celebratory scene. The red in this rainbow starts from this dead figure in the foreground of the mural, almost representing pooled blood as the red eventually joins the orange, then yellow, then other colors to create a brighter rainbow.

The rainbow continues into another scene on the right, the troublesome one. This is what I've been looking for. Here, in this scene, the World-War-II-era-gas-mask-wearing figure is not defeated. He's very alive, holding a sword in one hand and his machine gun in another, wearing vintage military garb in a way that makes him appear as if he is a menacing comic book figure of a bygone era.

To the viewer's left, the children are huddled and hiding, mere inches from his sword. On the other side of those children, an exodus of people painted in a way to depict a cycle of humankind (we've lived that before). Except here, the cycle in this scene that hangs to the right of hope is one of misery, the rainbow fades. A dove at the tip of this menace's sword looks like it barely is getting away.

It's not flying towards us, but headed towards something else.

The large figure who demands the focus of the eye, overtakes crumbling buildings opposite the human exodus and the children huddled in a ditch. I take several photos to capture that I found *it.*

I wonder if it is true about the tunnels beneath the airport? I carry with me the legends and stories about this place because of the bizarre artistic choices scattered throughout the airport. I don't rest eyes upon these spaces within the airport, but I know about them. The gaze of a gargoyle. The time capsule addressed to the people of Denver not to be opened until 2049.

For all the wonder that capsule alone has generated, will we have a hearty laugh because the cloak and dagger of it all will result in a hoax?

Or much like many places, will it be something that will make us wish we never wondered about it at all?

2B

Places call us back
Places pull us in

In the beginning, we are all enemies of our place of origin. The womb of Mother. We trick the uterus to take up residence, commandeering a body. Some of us exit on our own terms, but the many? We enter. We claim territory. We let whoever is in charge know that we are here and refuse to leave unless…

Can places be wombs that are hostile to us? Are those places that are either the welcoming or hostile wombs that way because of what we've done within them…to them…what we have done to each other?

What is the baggage claim on that?

Ireland has one of many examples. The place that holds within its soil how belief, body, and land clashed held within the lines of,

Are you a witch,
or are you a fairy?
Or are you the wife of Michael Cleary?

The back story to this nursery rhyme also tells of the friction between the belief in the Fae—I'm not talking about Disney's Tinker Bell—and the cultural shift towards modernity. Time was becoming current and the currents of this motion pushed a man to murder his wife. In 1895, Michael Cleary believed that his wife was not his wife at all, but overtaken by spirits, or fae, she'd encountered while working as a successful seamstress.

*

Some say, Lizzie Borden's house is such a place. Some say a few houses connected to the architect Frank Lloyd Wright might be pregnant with it.

And so is the Willows Weep house in Indiana.

The Indiana house that one can "read" as an upside down cross from an aerial shot (but only upside down for Christians, right?). The same house that has seen too much to contain life.

All the places as the hostile wombs that reject us.

Think: *American Horror Story* murder house, and all the real life
murder houses around the globe
Think: The mountain they say kills people with sound
Think: Aokigahara Forest

Do these places reject us or did we reject ourselves upon their soil and teach them how to continue to bathe us in our own venom?

*

Shirley Jackson knows the answer to this question of the paradox of place as cocoon. As hostile womb. As catacomb.

Shirley instructs that *place* and *safe* are oxymorons.

The familiarity of home. Children who disturb a mother or family with their behavior (they parade along the thinnest of veils between savage and domestic, don't they?). The neighbors and neighborhood who are the original liminal space that enmesh strangers, family, safety, and danger. The apartment building with a daemon lover who does and doesn't live there. That one individual, place, or thing who refuses ignoring and keeps appearing and disappearing to shift sane to unsane.

Maybe like people, we teach these places how to reject or accept the parasite known as us.

We will wish we never
wondered and wandered…

Does the soil become filled

bones unburied in Salem, MA

with the stench

Lawson blood blooms in

Germantown, NC
Madame Koi Koi's territory
Known and unknown mass burial sites
Gettysburg, PA
Himeji Catstle
Hinterkaifeck Farm
The Donner Party…

of death hysteria murder
human trauma?

But really, places eat you in exchange for the stories you tell about them

Let's be honest. Let's tell the truth about how American imagination, marketed and packaged by the Hippies, fashioned, painted, and implanted this place into all of us. Fed-the-us-that-did-not-exist-yet-us stories about different kinds of India.

Then there's the playscape of consciousness. A landscape of the colored caravan of monks. The monarch butterfly I saw months before the black and orange wings materialize upon arriving here.

How old was she?
And those howls? Did you hear them?
Did you notice how, even in the day, what the night hid seemed to pull, hold, and grip?
Did you hear them calling?
Did you wonder if it was one of the She's-Who-Shall-Not-Be-Named?

Did you picture her howling, calling, wanting us to know that She was squat, ready on her haunches, teaching us the way of this night, the way that only Mother can?

Did you hear the way She was telling us about how this place? The way this place can't be seen if you are afraid of being taken in, disappeared?

It was this place that warned me in my dreams that if I came to it, I'd return to America and tell the story, *"How,"*

How it ate a marriage.
How it ate the girl that was not yet a woman.
How it gnawed and christened the girl into woman.

Is a place searching for you long before you were ever conscious of it to hand you pieces of the self that you did not know were missing?

1B

Places are pain fields
Places are hurting fields that leave a trail
of breadcrumbs that leave our stomachs aching

Sometimes breadcrumbs start the trail to the place that never was.

Here is the assignment (get some sheets of paper and other materials): Build your dream house drawing floor plans to scale equipped with a diorama. Write a paper explaining the form and function of your dream home.

The stairs, they are double helix-shaped like DNA.
The outdoor pool, its defining feature is a mosaic at the bottom, something the girl wants from Greek Mythology (long before she understands the *what* she invites in through story).

The girl, she wants what she calls a "Me" room filled with the dolls she has collected. She wants a game room with Mario Brothers, Pac-Man, racing games…none of those games can be left out. The girl, she wants the living room sunken in (she's never seen one, doesn't know one, but figures that this just looks cool). She wants a kitchen with everything in it, "nice" as she describes it.

She needs a master bedroom with a balcony. She needs the house to be round (she knows nothing about Octagonal houses or at least, the former vogue for them). She needs her yard to look like a tangled, enchanted jungle like she is on the set of *The Secret Garden.*

A gate. Doesn't a house like this have a gate?
A view. Doesn't a house like this have a view? Why was the girl always looking at a forest or mass of trees?

She knows every doorknob. She knows every room. She has walked within a house that never existed. She continues to grow the rooms and details and designs on Pinterest. She now needs a sunroom and the herbal den. The girl knows the details of her kitchen and the bedroom.

If you built a place from the exact angle of the room to where you will the sun to come in to the number of stairs to the clean finish of the basement to the curve of the walkway, the question of hostility or welcoming are no longer, right?

That's all just place, the physical structures. But we never *really* talked soil. Does soil have owners?

If we build it, is it ours? If we choose it, is it ours?

Place: The Abridged Index

1A

Places are pain fields
Places are hurting fields

Or is it people hurt people and the
residue of these actions seep into
the soil of place?

2A

Places call us back
Places pull us in

But what about the places where
man crafts evil over and over and
over again in the shape of place?

3A

Places leave breadcrumbs out
of sequence and hidden in the body

Is following the breadcrumbs left
by a place worth your life?

4A

Places are unrequited
Places will break parts of you only for you
to want to break the barriers to re- enter them

Be. Careful. These are the best
and most horrendous ones

What is it about the venom of
place and sites of trauma that
call to us? Is it our own poison
drawing us in?

5A

Places train us up , mold us
Train our bodies how to move within them

Places that eat ashes and bodies
also eat other things
Places that eat ashes and bodies…
they are never full

5B

Places train us up as bodies are molded
and moved in the image of space

We know about places with no
bodies, what about bodies
without place?

4B

Places are unrequited:
You are always the one seeking out.
Be. Careful.

If you are seeking a place, was it always seeking you to hand you pieces of yourself?

3B

Places leave breadcrumbs
Places tell you to pay attention

Or much, like many places, will it be something that will make us wish we never wondered or wandered about it at all?

2B

Places call us back
Places pull us in

Can places be the wombs that are as hostile as our origin points?

1B

Places are pain fields
Places are hurting fields that leave
a trail of breadcrumbs that leave our
stomachs aching

Sometimes those breadcrumbs
start the trail to the place that
never was.

Parapraxic Dissociation: A Secret Instruction Guide

Also known as an instruction manual

How to Play in the Dark

There's the Bortle scale, 9 levels.*
There's my scale, 4 levels.

LEVEL 4

Familiar to all
You know what you see
I don't dwell here

LEVEL 3

Some witnesses
Even ones who pretend not to be witnesses
They might see
I hide
I seek

LEVEL 2

A dirt road
The part of the house
where the moon comes in
(just enough)
Just enough light to light a
beginning, but not all of it

The true start of play

*Inspired by the nine-point Bortle Scale which is a measure of the sky's light pollution/darkness within a given location.

LEVEL 1

One is indistinguishable
from another is
indistinguishable from me

No witnesses
I live here

1. Let me happen
   Let your skin adjust
   Let your eyes drink shadow
   Let shadow swallow your hearing

2. Why   you appear   ? And ?

   ?
   ?

   It is a summons,
   an invitation
   Don't you know how to answer when called?

3. Get yourself to stillness
   I am not within the binaural beat
   I am not within the mindful
   I am not within the Ommmmmmm
   I am not within the meditative state

   The uncomfortable
   I, the space between the question, the knowing
   that wraps around taking the swig of a tall glass of chards

   I am the prick that becomes the, "I need to feel that again,
   and again"

   The taste, metallic. Familiar.

4. Fully covered?
Shadows tickle the back of the throat?
In stillness that is undiscovered territory?

Good, good, now tell me

If this is all you had to dine—the chards, the shadow
ingestions through tallow—would you pay the fine?
Undid as should from the could that is
but couldn't because you wouldn't

5. It's more basic than #s
No metaphors

6. Start over

1. Adjust your eyes
The tensity of your neck
The tensity with subtle increase that goes

(you know it as sound in your chest mimicked in throat)

Those tensities, this is supposed to happen
Let me happen

2. Concrete not gravel
dirt follows street lights
now single street light

3. Now evergreens and the
ones that canopy
the skinny ones, the not-yet-ones
Now not full grown
high beams to low beams to
none—you better
for the full of it

4. 11:30 p.m. doesn't care about wonder

5. 11:50 p.m. doesn't care about why

6. 12:30 a.m. doesn't care about how

7. The key is about taking time
if it fits

You broke the rule:
Have the key ready
Always
Stumble? Fumble?
Not allowed

8. The walking is first

You broke the rule:
Parking in front of the door
creating shorter distance…that's cheating

But…you didn't run

9. The simple latch,
lack of lock
close the door
leave it like you let me happen
flip the latch

10. Lock all the doors
    Broken

    All the better for me to arrive without asking

    Lock Windows
    Broken

    All the better for me to come inside

11. Invite friends
    Even they have to leave

12. When alone, light the lamp, many lamps,
    for the one person who isn't inside

13. Let the light shine through the curtainless windows

14. Lit lamps…all the better for my eyes to see
    from the outside

15. Lights out
    count the steps from ground to up

16. Don't check the lock
    Don't check the open windows

17. Don't check the back door

18. Know that the emergency escape door wouldn't really work
    [the latch sticks, you must use a…]
    Know that your vehicle is parked in the front
    Know that you've taken the spade, the poker, the shovel,
    the fire tools, the gasoline to the mower is…
    Know that you have no idea about the noise
    from above that keeps occurring
    [the roof, nothing can really stick to it and there is no attic]
    Know that your fully charged phone has spotty cell service,
    the landline is downstairs [with the curtainless windows]
    Know that the neighbors said they don't have a phone
    or internet [didn't they brag about doing Pilates online?]
    Know that the *anyone* who could hear your scream within 1 mile
    won't say a peep because you and being here were never
    supposed to connect

19.

Sleep ✓
Solace ✓
Shotgun ✓

How to Play Mercy

I.

You end on your knees, but the procedures are simple.
Stand in front of another. Surrender yourself to them.
Surrender yourself to what will happen.

Mercy is the name of the game

Put your hands up. Right hand to their left hand. Left hand to their right hand. Palm to Palm. Fingers to Fingers. Clasped. It begins. both sets of hands in simultaneous pushed-pulled, one bent wrist meets bent wrist. Swept motion, knuckles now pointed to floor squirm, squirm, wiggle, knees buckled as if gripped as your hands are now gripped.

Mercy is the name of the game

At some point you end up on your knees looking up, screaming mercy.
At some point, you enjoy how well your lungs belted out the sound,
enjoy your wrist bent back, strained against itself. Enjoy the way
the eyes that brought you to your knees look down upon your body.

II.

You begin on your knees, and the instructions are simple.
Your right hand facing your left hand, palm to palm, fingers to fingers.
Pointed up to ceiling or sky, clasped with wrists locked.

You will repeat the word, *Mercy*
Embody *Surrender*
Repeat and be correct in form
Seek from a gaze from a sight unseen

While on your knees

You get off on the way you know you are the surrendered

III.

You begin on your belly, no knees involved.
Your hands, your wrists. Still.
Still as the air you control in your lungs. No move made,
you stay that way as fixed as air as you tricked yourself thinking . . .

You willed this
You are the one watching,
Observing . . . but really

IV.

For the sacroprofaned, it's straight forward
To stealth and stalk, one must be stalked
To observe, one must be the observed
To have every tip of toe bent to bend
air to stillness

How many toes, fingers, bones
will you part from body?

What will you bow, break, give
per pound of flesh?

Snap bone in trap
Make precise incision
Bring all pounds of meat
Crashed down to ground

How well can you expose a vein,
a self to a ready, willing, always opened
jaws, exposed throat?

How ready are your ankles, your muscles,
your gripped, ripped sinew, how ready are they
to bring you down to the ground to surrender?

V.

And for willing air to be that stabled, quiet
how long can you hold breath
Til you ain't your own no more?
Til your lungs beg, scream

release?

After all, you ain't think you were jus' gonna Come
See
Conquer
Take?

Preparations for Slaughter (I)

When a bear tells you he builds boxes
instead of dens for hibernation . . .
you've been warned

All kills begin with a conversation
We watch a sexed city tell a man *Kill me again*
He who arrives, not on horseback but in black town car

He who kills with wallet,
with penis,
with withholding

So good at this slay, his prey delivers herself
on a plate, sacrificial beast who taught us
how slaughter could be a voluntary, clean wanted and erotic act

Preparations for Slaughter (II)

I. 5 a.m., Thursday, October 20

Chewing takes sharpened teeth,   a strong jaw
Tightened jaw grips words   formed from leakage,
from slits of eyes that speak pounce   hands signal ready
Ready to pin the hunted,   grip air escaped from mouth

How this trains you for all the others   breath that tries to escape

when the bait becomes the baited
when weight of weight can't hold
when severed vocal cords never need blades
when snapped neck pon snapped neck pon
snapped neck needed no fur, no forest
to taunt this kind of hunt

II. 8 a.m. Thursday, October 20

Notice the prey, preferably a peripheral noticing.
If direct eyes must be involved, meet the gaze
directly. Be the first to turn away. Notice the pulse
in other parts of the body. The way the heart makes
the pelt rise and fall. Subtle. Notice the air caught on
sharp, hooked breath. See how it stops.
Notice when it is stilled.

This is the cue.

Notice the intimate nature of this space of the hunt,
profane space that is sacred space that is both.
Every moment of focus on the kingdom of the wanted,
hunted, lusted-after thing. Gaze fixed upon what invites
its tongue, its throat to swallow. Know what fills its belly.
Trained eye on its eyes, opened and closed in day, in dark.
Ear tuned to how all its limbs move. Nose fixed to how air
Announces, "NOW!" The way it reminds of all hours all
care all everythang trained upon the thing that will be the kill.

Understand the rules. This agreement made
upon eye contact with the eyes that spoke
pounce, get.

III. 3 p.m. Thursday, October 20

Know this, this is part of your existence
How all of you teases, taunts, tempts
How you and the thing that chases you
both understand the rules. Unspoken rules
They don't ask permission to chase

No consent ever given over to this chasing.
In this space of proscacrofanity, we agreed.

This. Just. Is.

IV. 5 a.m. Friday, October 21

There seems to be an unspoken agreement
My every breath caught in lungs, the way I've
been consumed by what I seek to consume . . .
Has this become my house of devotion?
My mantle of worship? This thing I hunt,
this thing I inhale . . . has it become my . . .

V. 3 p.m. Friday, October 21

No question . . . it rests in my marrow
sounds against bones, the ways they
stand above and beside me in declaration
How they've studied and steadied their gaze
How my pelt moves with what beats beneath
How I am theirs because of committed time
How I am gotten because when time was not
lookin' they tricked it to a stand still, laid seeds
and roots of a bloodless slaughter

The most insidious kind cuz the incision
is precise, the quick made kind, while caught in
in-between space, stood-still time and air
How a hand with folded, depth fingers enter
How they have a surety of how to reach
the heart with ease with the hand that knows
how to grab the heart, grip, squeeze, stop it,
stand still its pulse and leave without
spilling one drop of blood

VI. 11:30 p.m. Friday, October 21

Removing the pelt, the skin, exposing the raw meat?
Separating   severing   gripping   tearing sinew
from muscle from bone?

The proper preparation to chew?
                                        to swallow?

The hunters and the hunted—
they taught us about this part

To feed a corpse eater, you must . . .

Submit: The way you will shut your own eyes   cover them
Cover your own ears. Fold in on yourself
The quiet within the folding mimics mama's womb

Or it's the names of God
Or it's how others, just like you, are present
(*the kill is less nervous that way*)

The calm of your surrender is the stuff of legend

This is how

Presentation: Place body on butcher block   with your own hands
Expose your own neck, your belly
With your own hands, give the blade its instruction

They teach you

Be the digested thing: Feed the corpse eater   with your flesh
Rest in the Slaymaker's belly. Be the dead
thing a thing well - done, a died thing

To want it . . . The Slaughter

You're the kill who wants to be the kill
This is how they taught you . . . the wanting
They still tell about the way you enjoyed
About the way you smiled wide in imagined
glory while rested in their marrow. To all who hear this
story, you are the profaned that became sacred
because . . .

who wouldn't want that?

How Do I Know You're Not Inviting Me To A Murder?

Exhibit A

I never picked a weapon
but here we were

standing

This dead body surrounding us
I guess by saying nothing

it's picking by default

I thought that not picking
it meant not guilty

it meant

Not an accomplice because
accomplices pick weapons of choice,

right?

Exhibit B

It's Mary, or Liselle, or Lisa or somebody you claim to be as you ask

Are you free tomorrow?

Or it starts with "Hello" or it starts with "How are you?" followed by the unwanted pic. To end the game of texting with strangers, I tap my weirdo-close-to-the-surface-weird

Who is this? I don't know this number…

you might be inviting me to my murder.

Hello is no longer the beginning of trepidation.
This time you give me an address.
This time, I pretend I am the one you were looking for.
This time,

Exhibit C

Before it had the name, it was food
Catfish was preferably fried
Even better, blackened.
It was a dish, never a thing a person would do

Exhibit D

It was just a game of hypergamy dodgeball with one inside joke, "Gurrrrrl, don't roll up and get murdered." It was "Gurrrrl, send his address" or you just knew better because the first thing you notice is the pic, the edges, like someone else is cut out of it.

That didn't do it

The hair, the glasses, shades, you can't see his eyes
and this is the only photo on the profile

Maybe this didn't do it

It was the offer veiled as an invitation camouflaged, as in
permission would not be granted but barriers were crossed

Come over
We will have dinner
I will rub you
I will, you will…we

How many paragraphs did it take to realize that the invitation
was the offer to a future rape in progress?

Exhibit E

Catfish can change their gender
They can blend in with muddy water
They can look like rocks
They can swim upside down in deep water
The bellies offer more protection that way

Exhibit F

It was some kind of holiday the night we chose to drive from CT to DC at 4 p.m. in the afternoon. No hotel needed. Blend in as hotel guests, *stay in a friend-not-really-a-friend's-room.* We get dressed. We pull up to the club. *We never agreed on the club or the celebration.* You and me choose to walk the streets. *What was it about our middle of the night walks always from where we were supposed to be?*

Your belly exposed, my breasts barely covered, and our companion somewhere in the middle. We were in the middle of crossing the street when some version of a Maybach pulled up.

Of course we got in.

Of course we made jokes about him driving us to an undisclosed location with friends waiting to hurt and maim.
Of course you sit in the front seat, our giddy fueling your giddy
Of course…all of us filled with, "Our parents would beat the living shit outta us."

Parents beating us kept company with the bigger never-to-be-recovered-from-kind of beating.

Severed vocal cords. Missing persons never found. The milk cartons we knew well with "Have you seen" went missing in this moment.

What was it about edges & the way we courted them?
What was it about needing to know how deep that kind
of cut could go?

Exhibit G

Pangasius Bocourti
Silurus Glanis
Pangasius
Octocinclus

If you count all the kinds,
they are 10.8% in biomass
They are 1 in 20 of animals, of all vertebrates
They are 1 in 10 of all fish species
They are the over 3000 catfish species
Catfish…they are everywhere

Exhibit H

The Restaurant. Your apartment. The U-Haul Van. The rest stop.
The way we drove away from that place with the car full of dudes
following us (they were coming too).

That window with the shades that part slightly with no face ever present
(it was the same time every day on the walk from high school).
That time you said that the government was after you in between long
conversations. You were careful to stay on certain streets (come to think
about it, driving around with a minor could not be a thing. Maybe the
wife seeing you with said minor could not be a thing).

If unsolved mysteries taught us anything, it was a lesson about how anywhere is the scene of a crime. If the wrong man taught us anything, it was about the warning he gives for all his kind when he tells you:

You are the perfect candidate to make a man kill you.

Exhibit I

A catfish can traverse land
Up to 2 miles on a good day
Up to 18 hours on a humid or rainy day

A catfish lays eggs
on top of other fish eggs
Their children hatch and murder the others
Their borrowed mother knows no difference

Exhibit J

You watch *No Country for Old Men*, the same movie that Javier Bardem turns down for 3 reasons:

1. He does not care for violence
2. He said his English was so-so at the time
3. (You don't remember the third reason and what if 1 and 2 are not true?)

Exhibit K

Do you see him on the screen?
Does he remind you of someone?

Parapraxic Dissociations From Safe Spaces

Run, run. Run left off Harold onto Palm where the store is no longer
Run past the Hughes House on the corner, I know it is theirs.
Run, run, we found a clawfoot. Stay still as someone tries the bathroom door. Can't see their faces. Can't they see us? The edges of the clawfoot won't hide us. The top around the clawfoot has no lip.

Scooch, scooch, down down low. No matter how far down.
Scooch, scooch, we accordion our bodies, but the clawfoot tub…
it refuses to hide us.

Like the Basement,

a space that refuses to hide from you. You wanted to know it, and yet. you didn't. Yet, you never wanted to venture down into it because it looks like that place. You know that place I'm talking about. It's always the same place. A damned place. The one with the stairs that descend further into the *it* you've been courting and avoiding. You will keep avoiding this same place for years, into adulthood.

The basement is…sometimes finished with that cheap area carpet. Sometimes it has those plain tile floors and is lined with lockers. Never brightly lit, which begs the question: Who and what are all the shadows? What's in those boxes against the wall? What's in all those lockers?

You ever meet a basement you didn't want to know? That time and all those other times, even now…you just stay at the top of the stairs. Sometimes you will stay thinking about how a few minutes changes what it feels like now. But you stay at the top of the stairs because…

It didn't feel right during the tour of that one school. There, you see it. Not quite basement level, but not quite above level either. They tell you it is the place where everyone gathers, but the lights are off when you see it. No bodies are in there now.

It's the place you know better with your eyes closed and you know better than to cross the threshold.

Speaking of knowing better, my cousin's hand me downs attracted strangers

The blue was too bright, baby blue borderline peppermint. I hated it, the hand me downs of my cousins. I long stopped getting allowance so sometimes I told my parents that the bus broke down so I could theft the fare and walk. With the bus fare, I'd buy a bag of cheese doodles and a chubby juice. The twenty five cent kind.

I'd walk down past the abandoned showroom that long stopped having cars in it. I'd pass the yellow brick abandoned factory. The one that had one store left in it. The one building that was topped with a fading smiling face. Nobody ever knew what that store sold.

Pass that long row of red, the brick building with the *Salvation Army* sign. The unending, unbroken building on the right with one long row of traffic on the left that never leaves but just seems to sit, even when the light turns the color of one of those peppermint, clear candies.

The day of the too baby too bright for that blue, the fading smiling face on the building that was disappearing yellow was in view. Almost there when she stops me, she demands to know, *Do you want something to happen to you?* Her eyes hid behind black shades. Her body unhidden by any coat. Hands wrapped around arms—she hugs herself in the way her hair refuses to hug the face with the voice that demands, *Do. You. Want. Something.To.Happen.To.You?* The traffic does what it always does along with the fading smiling face atop the faded yellow brick. They…the traffic and the smiling face…see everything. But,

they don't see us.

They don't see the way I shake my head *no* in slow motion because the stranger's shades and body took my voice. They don't see the way the coatless stranger hugging herself makes her body wrong. Shoulders too pointy and her body, folding in, narrowing. They don't know I refused her my body.

My coat refused my mind to wander on a wonder about her eyes behind the shades. And memory does that—this coatless woman with the narrowing body and pointed shoulders that day and the too baby, too bright for that blue forever mortgage free, keeps silence with an occasional question:

She wants to know if I am still a good girl, the kind of girl who wants something to happen.

What was the something?

And good girls who want something to happen? You'd be surprised

It's always best to disappear bodies when the sun deprives us of a viewing and when the rain can't even be bothered to show up. Instead, it drizzles here, there…confused about location, like the sun that day. These kindz of days treat doin wrong like all the good stuff that settles to the bottom of a cup. She was the good stuff and she didn't know that I'd be the bamboo stirrer.

It was horror movie perfect.
I needed directions.
She was in no rush.
I was unassuming.
She was taught to assume nothing.
So, the answer is always ignore the shovel in the back seat. Accept the invitation, the call to be good. Answer the question. *Directions?*

Didn't know blood could splatter like that.
Didn't know that hair was so persistent.
Didn't she realize in this day and age….

We stopped giving directions
to people in cars.

To Be Continued…

Proverbs for Surviving Insanity Cross Dressed As Sanity

1. Sanity and Normal
   Sanity and normal are illusions (but we can't tell anyone)

2. Reality
   They keep arguing about the simulation of things, if this is real, what would happen if we discovered that it isn't. It's simple and it's complicated. We keep playing *Sims* and wear an Oculus while entering Meta to figure it out.

3. The Reanimation of Your Childhood
   When you see your childhood reanimated—cartoons now movies now whole ass revival—remember you barely made it out that other time.

40. On Entering Murder Houses
    Speak from the deep of the belly, the diaphragm. No need to climb the gate, it'll open. If you go inside, warn everyone, they must stay in groups, especially where you see the double staircase, the one on the left and the one on the right surrounded by marble. The marble is the most beautiful part of the house. When you are in this part, don't leave each other. The house, it plays tricks.

58. Slow Cars
    Slow driving cars, the ones that are not looking for a destination or target, but the ones who are roaming? Listen to the way the tire consumes the dirt, the gravel. Notice the full-term pregnancy of the stop and how the engine stays on.

    A long, healthy low hum. All out of sight and if all is true, ask: How long will it take for it...this sound of waiting to go away?

61. Holding Strange Babies

You'll meet a baby on your lap that you end up holding, but you're not sure how it got there. Maybe it's your kid. Maybe you're the baby, sitting. Maybe none of these things. When you meet this baby, if you trip while holding him, cover it wholly. Cover it with your body. Make sure it is not harmed. Make sure this baby knows nothing of what is happening around him. Your body will take the blow. But his body, the baby's body, must never touch the concrete. His father is watching.

103. When you meet leopard cubs

of varying ages, it is your moral duty to take them with you. No, this is not 1938's *Bringing Up Baby*. No Carry Grant. No Katherine Hepburn. This will happen before you know that such a thing exists. So when you meet these leopards, take them to a hotel room. Their jaws will open with no sound. You will teach them that they can roar. They can make sound. For these, these are feral thangs.

115.

If you find yourself on any road, find the roots of the trees. Stay along the margin of the tree roots and run. Don't stop because stopping means you will be discovered.

128.

We promise this. Remember, sleep in a comfortable place. Opening your eyes will take time, they won't at won't at first, open that is. Be patient.

400.

Don't ever *think* you aren't being watched (we don't mean in the digital sense). When you see vacant windows, vacant cars, know you are watched. When silence bathes you, your body (alone they call it?), you are being watched. And how do we behave under the all seeing?

How will you be while being watched?

Memory Works Like Jumping from Julian to Gregorian What About That Manor?

Epilogue

A woman is the last to join a group of travelers on a patio. None of them know each other.
A woman chooses one of the patio chairs at one of the tables, the one closest to the main office. None of the travelers look in her direction. They are too busy talking and giggling. A woman orders chai and then pretends to read her book.

A woman waits for a pause in between the space of laughter and words. A woman picks a target. The table to the left. The easiest table because they are close. A woman starts the conversation,

Do any of you know about the place in the back?

No…wait…maybe

A woman spends the next hour telling them about where she stayed. The conversation grows into an exchange of stories among tourists. These tourists leave.

The woman decides to tell the office
The woman asks about the man, the one who helped her last night. One of the desk attendants she's seen before looks at her strange and insists that they closed early because the rooms were booked.
The woman describes the man. His smile. His hair. His approximate height. She then describes the manor and he responds,

We know the place.
We never rent it   to anyone

It's been closed for renovations for years.

About M.M. Jones

M.M. Jones takes breaks from their music projects to explore experimentation in their writing while occasionally manipulating the places, people, and things they encased within the images they create . With blood that flows in all directions of the Mason—Dixon line, Jones's music and writing, contain the obsessions of place. Most specifically, place as its own entity that sometimes becomes caught up in human drama.

M.M. Jones is collaborating with Shanta Lee on a short run of murder ballads to accompany *Do Words Dream Themselves Into Silence Told In Riddles?* (Harbor Editions, 2026).

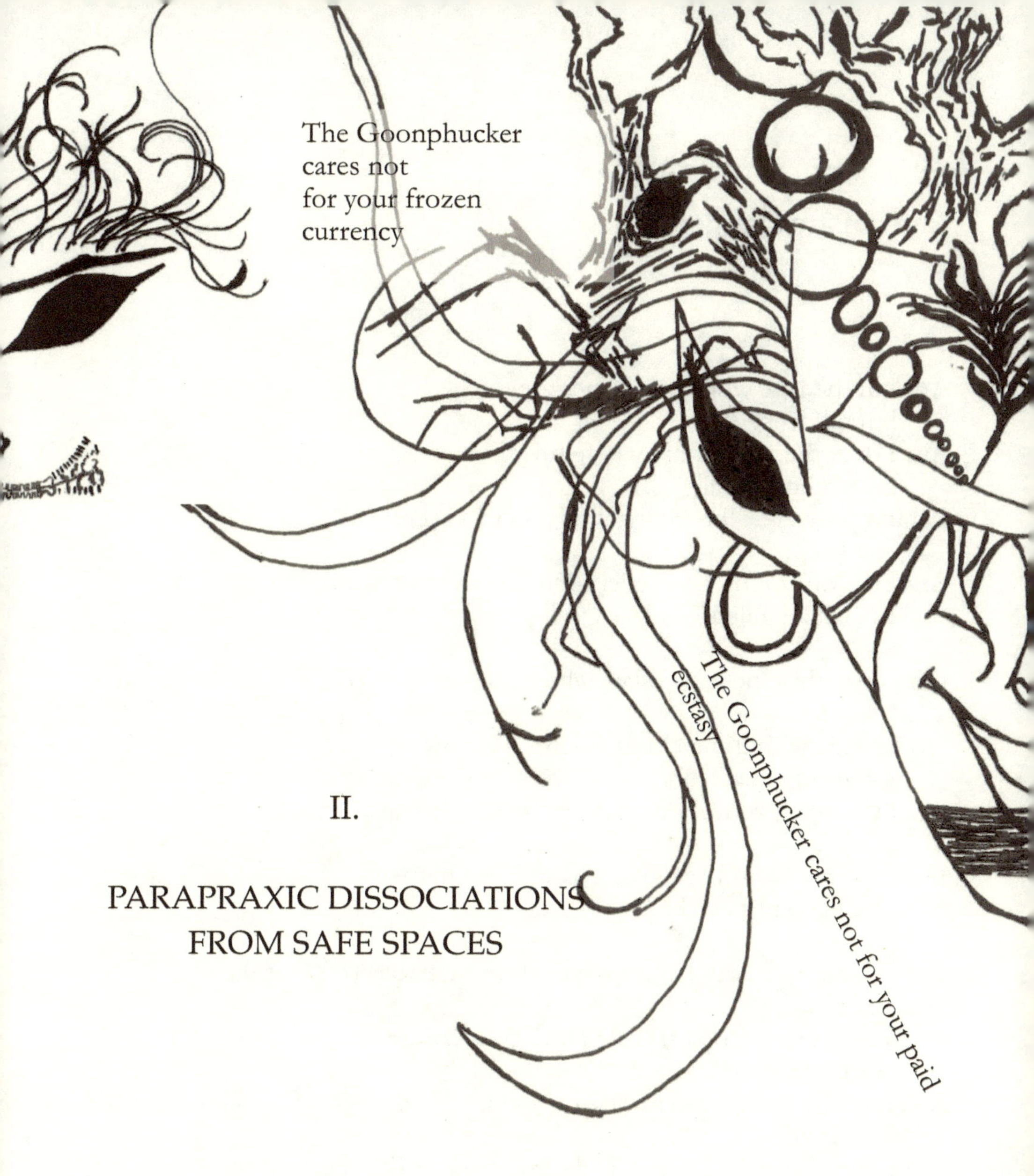

II.

PARAPRAXIC DISSOCIATIONS FROM SAFE SPACES

The Goonphucker loves the cryptocryobinge
he laughs at everywhere you've been

Catechistic Danger

Am I in the lake where my bones are
    buried deep?
Am I over the sunrise hill where my
    breath holds still?
Behind your eyes, lids kept shut, is there a secret that
    you keep?
Am I the one who's been tricked? Am I the one who's life
    has been spilled?

Do I lie within the wood slats where you see the red
    seep through?
Do I reside within the closet where all of my
    things stay packed?
Dare you open your mouth wider than day to taste what
    is true?
Dare you will your tongue to savor how a human
    life becomes cracked?

Is he an entity? Does he live near? Have they told you that they
    are holy?
Is it a neighbor turned friend? Have they claimed to be
    a simple man?
You let them inside, attention get got? Under the veil of good time
    and jolly?
Have they started a story to make you forget? Do you hear the
    alphabet of how it began?

Hear me now, heed me good
Hear how this is going to end
Hear the hushhhh, open to yessss and nowww—understood?
Here, stay here, be present with me, gimme your whole body
let's again begin.

You Know The Dead

don't just ooze from sockets
of a caught thing, a dead thing,
but from something still   alive

Teetering on edge between known
and unknown place . . . I knew a dead-live
caught thing when I glimpsed it

Sometimes that seepage ain't
from a dead-other thing but from
the caught-dead-live-walking-live thing

The thing that thought it was
the catcher, the hunter, the bricklayer,
the dead-live walkin' thang,

but really, jus' a walking dead
who's not realized they paved
a road to worship where obsession is focus

And to obsess a thing like that,
stalk a thing like that, dare tingle
your tongue for it . . . dare ingest it . . .

You can't say we didn't warn
about how the ache to consume
will end yuh

When the Emaciated, Starved God Becomes

Knuckles ache, fingers cramped. Broken bones cackle and crack SNAP! SNAP! nails bent back. Rough. Soiled. Never cleaned hands wrapped round ankles. My hands, they rake this soil in hopes that another will see shallow tracks, disturbed dirt, play close attention to where a body has been. Of where the one who has been here and one who wasn't. See the fingers that overworked a garden. Search for flesh under nails that passes as dirt because some flesh folds with night, some flesh folds with dirt.

> Tune your ears for distinct pitch, run yourself ragged
> findin me, bend your body to my baying. I've been
> captured. I've been scattered.

Emaciated,
    Starved god, has sought flesh and soul
    to hallow the hollow belly, I am digested whole

Emaciated,
    Dissolving insatiable god who's feasted
    and famined all things, what do you demand
    leaving more sacrificial sprawl

Hunger might be about some
semblance of filling yourself.
Feeding the empty. Some
semblance of contentment. But
the Emaciated, starved god, the
dissolving god…it will drag a
body. It will use it to build its
house. It will take up residence.

Steps for Self-Immolation (Not to Be Tried at Home)

1. Self-immolation was a promise if we go to the glorified dollar store. The one always going out of business, but this time, they are open.

2. Dolls stock the shelves, they are declared beautiful. They have beer, they have pretzels, they have a healthy vending machine (healthy, can you believe it?)

3. They have kayaks but no paddles. They have clothes…well… some. There's soap. There's toothpaste but no candles. The lights? Not annoying fluorescent but dull. It's time to ask the clerk.

4. I tell the clerk, *I never knew these kinds of stores, the glorified dollar stores, existed in other countries.*

5. I checked out, but can't leave this country.

6. I checked out but they don't believe that my passport's still at the hotel. The one where the clerk always kept the lights out. The one with the desk that takes everything that goes into it.

7. This clerk and the other clerk….and the other clerks, they need to know.

8. Self-immolation is a promise if I don't leave.

Does the Body Dream Itself Into the Maze It Can't Escape?

The 400lb Butcher on the abandoned farm he's gonna fix my kickstand

& the Nissan Maxima is still covered in blood & the voice of a man
continues to chase

he will steal, he will harm

& the white tip of the building in the distance is home & my best
friend hides her baby

refuses his face from my eyes

& the grandmother whispers into your ear this from her grandson,

This is the conversation I've been
having with my negro girlfriend

& an enigmatic jigsaw breaks skin from left to right

& the couple that keeps watch over me making sure I
don't leave (just remember to hide the keys)

& the Platypuses that deceive on all fours then spring up
to chase they will catch us, catch us soon

It's been so long since I've been home. I do not want to ruin the longing of gone and missing, so leave it. Leave it like frankincense.

.~ You tell me in a letter, *Regardless of all the things in life, we're all just bodies, showing up.*

.~ You remind me that the last time we all hung out, we weren't born yet. *Remember,* you said, *You must live. Leave.* Where was I going? What was I leaving?

.~ Leave like those words they stopped me from saying. I was trying to tell a story. They stopped me with voices growling loud and screaming as we stood on the sidewalk while their eyes said, *We are saving you from saying. You can't say what you should not.*

.~ A vanilla bean girl comes apart in pieces, disintegrates in front of us. It's time to explain ourselves. *Give them,* the Butcher instructs, *a body to destroy. And go to where the Tunnel People are.*

ᛚ

The tunnel people, the Butcher warns, *don't speak statements.*
I'll train you in questions,

If a woman leaves a note telling a piece of her story like a riddle, am I her hype man? Am I telling the crowd, *You have to listen to this. You won't believe this,* as she tells what they made her do?

If highlighted text creates shapes with the letters, which are the found words by the author [?] Which ones are the made-up words [?]
Will I know what other parts are a lie [?]

Where is the hourglass, the right one, the one that keeps time slow [?]

How can I escape from a human shapeshifter [?] The one that snaps necks coming for me next [?]

Are all the mothers coming home to roost [?]

ᚠ

Her story is the riddle she uses to hold the room,
You won't believe this. Listen…

There are womens who are dressed in black. They will come regularly. Listen, if you play too close to the edges, you won't get any of the wool. Listen, if you see the deep red bannisters, the deep red stairs, this is a wood structure. You only enter cemented places.

Listen, she says
Listen, I mimic
saw we do
see

ᚠ

Know the Butcher, he will never fix your kickstand

& I'm crouched down on the car floor, been stuck there for days. For days, the car window is open carrying their voices. Their threats are promises, *We promise to mess you up.*

& No one passes through to help you, speaks the dirt on the road that leads to the farm.

& I soothe myself with the tellings. I hand myself reminders in the way of the riddle in the language of the Butcher

& She-Who-Holds-Rooms with enigmas

& I've learned their language

II

First, notice the music

Fishnets, black pantyhose
Don't start moving or bopping around.
Just notice.

Second, notice the food, the Cajun dressing that
also camouflages as Ranch. There are different
kinds and you know its Cajun because of what it
says…

Third, an animal chooses you,
you don't ever choose them

Fourth, start swaying
then bopping
then move your feet
it's infectious

& then there's the Preacher's Daughter
Preacher's Daughter looks familiar
Her voice screams me down askin,

Why did you come here?

Doing Time in the Place Where We Are Going to Next

Sometimes when you are doing
a certain kind of time—No thing
makes sense.

Making sense or logic stops being the goal.

Not the back
but the side

Through the bile

broke glass. Sent for. You. Be.

*

Thumbtacks, but first, heat them
The knife? The sharp one…
new new sharp

Bookcase. Carved.
Severed.
Blood pulled and zigzag

This way that
Rhymed, nursed….See

*

My daughter, eyes of onyx
My daughter, a fat Buddha's laugh
My daughter, she....
Missing
Gone
Not missed My bastard
belongs to the
zippered-faced-man

*

The door knocks itself
But you speak no English
The door needs an answer

Are you the girl of onyx eyes?
You follow the zig-zagged red?

You speak...
where did you kidnap my scarf?

*

Heel. Toe. Heel. Toe. Heal. Toe
Don't walk them shoes on no wood
They will hear you comin'

*

What did it sound like? Behind the doors
that cooled our backs led straight to Bates's long dead?

How did you know to go to Jerusha?
That grave isn't even standing…

The moon looks good on our bodies
We sit where we are gonna be soon

in planet years

We clean Jerusha's stone
Take fall's seed off of her

She likes that

We wonder, we ask: Why is her head at her lover's feet?

This is why she may be pissed

*

The colored crayons imprinted on the wall,
you must know how to read the wall

__________, 10

__________, 14

__________, 17

These are not the heights of the children,
these are the ages from bottom to ceiling

*

Put her in the fire
(because that's what she wanted)

Take her breath with a pillow
(because that's what she wants)

Fill her with food,
(because that's what she wants)

Drown her in the toilet bowl
(give it to her)

She wants release and ease
from why it feels like this

*

The only ones who are swimming are drowning

Suicide By

Proxy

My body beats dawn
My wrist ache but the cow calls,
the goats bleat
My wrist crafting miracles in morning's air
beating fresh cream to butter

The bread for my house, my husband, and the neighbors
won't bake itself
The new babe won't swaddle itself nor quiet itself
The laundry can't beat itself against the rocks,
it can't deliver itself to the customers
The family tax bills loom
The lunch, the dinner, the chores, they can't do themselves

Did I finish the 20th prayer of the day?

My body beats dawn
My wrists, aches. The cow calls.
The goats bleat
My wrists, crafting miracles in morning's air,
I beat fresh cream to butter

Die Schwigermama comes
Die Schwigermama reminds:

> A babe is swaddled everyday for 4 months to be sure
> an extra one for luck
> The laundry is done best with both arms to beat the fabric
> Don't talk to Hans, his family is unlucky
> Don't talk to Inga, she has no husband and no children
> You have enough cream to sell butter as you
> sell laundering as you sell baking loaves girl
> You need to pay your part, taxes are due girl
>
> As for your pots, as for your pans,
> they won't keep themselves unscathed, unscratched
> As for your prayers? My son likes at least a dozen said
> over stirred pot girl

Did I do the 12 prayers over the stew?
Did I get enough well water for the week?

My body beats dawn
My aching wrists…the cow calls and bleating goats don't care
My wrists must do the work
beating cream to butter in morning's air

In morning's air,
3000 paces to fetch well water
for the week
By noon's yawn, the babe
quieted
2 loaves of bread,
baked

Keep the pans hung
as die schwiegermama said

The 12 prayers over the dinner pot,
as die schwiegermama said

as die schwiegermama says
as die schwiegermama says, as hausvater says,
as the man of God says,

A good wife is a moral wife
is a husband's safe and Godly home

Did I tend the family plot and pull the weeds?
Did I ask for God to keep my womb full?
Did I finish my prayers? Did I swaddle the baby
tight enough to avoid misshaping? Did I thank God for
home, hearth, and husband?

I've not seen my hair since I became his wife
I've not seen mum's hebane, the cloth wrapped mandrake root,
the _________ since leaving mum's home
I've not seen my friends from the old village

The fire smells different
like my herbs now feed the flames
The village, the people, they only celebrated
that night but no one comes to visit
The babe looks off
The goat seems still
The cow's milk does not produce enough cream for butter

Now I remember,
that look in his eyes when he told Baltzer,
You are handsome his arm folded around
his neck that night we wed

Now I remember,
Baltzer hanging himself after we wed
His eyes, my husband's eyes,
they were never the same

Now that I remember,
die schwiengermama undid my braid
die schwiengermama covered my hair, aproned me,
handed me the plastic baby

Do not shame my son's home,
You are now that home
Do not shame my son's children
You are now their mother

Now,
I remember
Labor started on the day of the wedding
I brought him the cart of chickens
I brought him other wares

Now I remember that I can't remember myself

Did I ask God, beg God
often, daily to fill my belly
Did I shame my home?

Did I kill our goat?
Did I sicken our babe? Our crops?

Did I dry our cow? Did I cause the fish not to come? Did I cause the whispers that threaten our hearth? Our roof?

Did I Did I

Did I

Did I

My body beats dawn
No goat bleats No bread to bake neighborsNo other laundry
but our own No cow calls
Nooutsideworkcallsthesehands

My wristmy hands every part of my body
must craft
miracles my breast milk

won'twhipintobutter

As we lay last night and he says its my fault our roof is taken
As we lay tonight, he says its my fault the stove is smashed
because *Men, they must not be run by their wives*
Die Schwiegermama says I did it

He says I'm the reason for all of it

My body beats dawn, for I am weary, tall weeds cover me I lay as still
as mybabeasmygoatiwatch the children iwaitiwaitiwaitwatch

Mutercallsigathercryingbabesolikemyownnottomybosomibringthebabe
tothenearestfallthisbabeasmybodyasmysoul

is tired, is weary

And I know that I must report myself,
I am the murderess

And I know that the village will gather,
and dance as my headless body sprouts

enough blood for bowls and cups for drinking
Die schwiegermama will get her helping

This will be one of the only times we lock eyes
as I gaze you from the executioned chair

from the cage that holds my head
The familiar path of your dry tears

The familiar feeling of you filling with worry,
familiar dread replaces your organs

Doesn't all of this remind you of our wedding celebration?

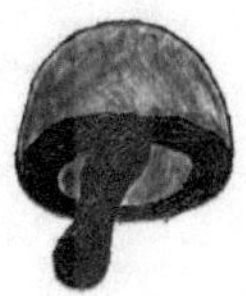

~~Suicide by~~ Sacrifice

It is not merely giving something up
And it is not merely weary

It goes beyond giving up anything
It is not about the glass
or hands that count linear
and it was never a story
I could tell you ~~the story but~~
you won't understand
When disease comes
When the Great Spirit is angered
When the bones of our brothers
and sisters stack and stack

Logic was never just about the head
Love isn't in the words
Living exists beyond this plane
When the sweat lodge does not cure
When the medicine dance does not calm
Go fetch my horse & lead him off the rock's edge
Find a place to bind me with all the things of war

I will gather those things
I will get on my horse
I will ride

I could tell, but you can't hold
How the knife felt going into my skull
the real cure for the ache
How there is no translateable language
for the feeling of lifeless limbs
of your brothers, sisters, wives, children

What does one do when so many parts of you vanish?
What does one do when you and the disease are seen as one?

What does one do but blind the horses and mount them?
Let them take us to the other plane
Let them take us to where
a heart
a spirit
a soul

Can be whole

But this IS the story

When the first one went, we knew it was her time to see the ancestors. We started to question when five young, healthy ones left followed by the medicine men followed by women. More children. It was disease, a disease the lodge could not cure.

More kept going while few remained to dance. The warriors were among the last ones until the last one drove a hatchet into his own head after seeing movement of the little ones from the next plane. And we can't stop what must, the angered Great Spirit must be appeased. Six Crow boys and six Crow girls, the ones who were carried away to continue our life.

They will tell the story.

But stories are workings. Stories are seeds, only certain kinds are carried by a wind that will erase some and plant others to bloom new crops. You are going to hear that it really went like this:

1. Two young Crow becoming men return home.

2. They return from their rite of passage to find all family gone.

3. Among their families included the sweetheart of one, the wife and baby of another.

4. In this version of the story that will be called a legend, the two never talk.

5. In this version of the legend, the two never consent to this agreement:

   Best to end ourselves than succumb to this.

6. In this version, there are 4 noted silences:

   The first silence is the silence of contemplation from their mountain time.

   The second is the interstitial silence of leaving who and what they were before while journeying and returning to who they are now.

   A third silence is the silence of the horror. Seeing all of the bodies and the one elder who was well enough to say,
   Do not come in.

   The last and fourth silence was described by some who will say it was the loudest. The quiet of the after. The *what must.....Must* kind of silence.

   It is in this quiet with the weight of a self-splitting heart, too heavy to be called any kind of broken, that one knows what must be done.

7. Modern language, fancy academic language, those who are not of us language, do not apply. Suicide: A colonizer's lexicon.

8. Or sometimes, it is the only word that makes sense but lacks all context.

9. In the howl of the after, the two young Crow blindfolded the horses and rode off the cliff.

10. The cliff is the one with the highest peak.

11. At least they gave it the name, Sacrifice Cliff, not Suicide Cliff.

Suicide by Sacrifice

Lives with several children that are
scattered so all parts of the story does not
know its kin. The real story of what
happened says to the readers:

Can you believe anyone or anything who
calls this truth a "legend"?

Can you believe anyone or anything that
uses the word "story" for what happened
here?

You will love the love story of it all. You
will want to visit for the photo opp of it all.

Thus, we won't bother telling you this
once long lost, now recovered version of
the story.

Green, Glass & The Nightgown That Growls

In a house of green and glass it happens once
Once is all it takes to land in a patient gown

The nightgown demands *Go stand outside*

[But won't I look like I'm a patient?]

The nightgown growls *This is good for you*
Stand on the corner
of Sherman

Am I with *them*?
Am I one of *them*?

I refuse the answer, normal clothes on my body
my body on the back of a motorcycle

The escape is icy slick Go!

Away from the house of green, the house of glass
the house that holds my patient room

GO!

The flat turned hill with ice, away from the gown that demands
The little boy on the tricycle unseen, the breaks pumped

Air on my body all say

I AM REAL

Under Gibbous Moon Eclipsed

Bring me to the house in the field
That one with rusted door, no knob, no windows
As the moon blinks and folds
A man with no face gestures, *Come*
The stone girl and boy refuse to watch
Instead they see the ones who refuse to leave

Come is an order, not invitation
Nor is the house missing the basketball hoop
Nor do the windows miss the signs of life
Nor is the street that is stilled under gibbous
Nor the faceless man with back bowed,
forming   threatening backflips
Nor is the partial skin of a face missing eyes
yet with parted familiar mouth stuck on the ground
Nor is the desk nearby that waits for a student
in empty factory lots

Under a full blood moon

find the missing baby in my baby picture
she is my daughter
Travel south in brief sunshine
let one minute eat 8 miles
Find the classroom in a maze of a building
and take a test, a failing test then tell him,
him whose desk rises high into the ceiling,

I can take another. I can do the extra work.

Under day's gaze,
bald tires of the Nissan reveals something
The Bodega has a phone
The auto shop owner is sensitive
refusing to tow the Nissan
People, the Bodega, and the
Bald-Tired-Nissan become
another world as I walk
A scorched, burned abandoned
apartment building intrudes
I turn east, south, and north with
my feet There is no avoiding
this place that grows

Hunger: An Origin Story

It was summer maybe. Maybe they walked because mama liked to walk and she thought her two-year-old needed a snack.

That two-year-old had other thoughts

They walked with the sun kissing Mama's petite frame. Mama in hot pants and halter also wearing some kind of shoulder length wig same as she wore in the picture wearing pink sitting next to Papa with that lil gurl in between.

The sun kissed, chubby limbs stumbling next to her mama. Mama didn't really do the stroller get up, not on these ragged walkways that were really mama's runways.

Lil gurl, in some kind of makeshift halter, little shorts, the velcro-little-kid-sandals, her small chunky toes peeping out

Lil gurl and her mama…they kinda matched

When they enter Parker's Drug Mama has a snack in mind

Lil gurl did too

The boy, that one, the one with a head full of curls, the color of the figs and newton Mama liked to feed lil gurl.

The boy, that one with the osh my gosh jean overalls just a little taller
than lil gurl. She goes to him, her clumsy walk, baby chunked
arms outstretched. Lips ready to lay one on

He moved
Or her mama stopped her
Or her mama yanked her back

Lil gurl's head kisses a counter instead
Lips never connected to the boy

Lil gurl now woman walks backwards to that spot, to that time in Parker's Drugstore reconstructing the giggles and smiles stitched into the family fable, *Memba that time, you tried to kiss a boy*

that explains why hair refuses to grow
in that area on that brow

Saliva and pressed lips traded for blood, lust traded for stitches with no playdate attached. Lil gurl now woman focuses on the retelling, she's more interested in the crime scene. How does a tongue become a trained thing to ride the dark of certain wounds? How does one tend the soil of want unfurling across a body?

She tells herself this is an origin stor…

All wrong questions
Little girls ain't spos'd
to know such things

A. We were all in that other place, sleeping. Spirit Chasers, Gunslingers, Dream Trippers, Tally Tilterbenders, Liminal-Twixt-Boardaries-And-Not Jumpers, Blind Sorcerers, Marauders, Immortal Maroons-From-All-Worlds, Apothecarians…all the who lived their point of no return. Turtle island was old, but young to all us. We had to be sleeping dreaming of this now.

Q. When did you know?

A. In opium dens, when your eyes are really closed.

Q. When???

A. Between staying in and going from his lap. Between being in and out of that place and the one that never is folding the hours, stretching the seconds in the space, where breath extended dodges day, refusing to know its name, refusing to know its hour, or the vibration of the thing. Rejection of the weight of can't say.

Those lumped throats are the beats that can't be swallowed they rock you the way a wave knocks a ship…

How long can I?

Q. The body is the dam, the dam holds it in, girl…
Gurrrlllllllllll, watcha hold?

A. The sickening.

I keep going back and back…

the way they talk about dope sick, or the way some things out dope the do…

A. Gurlllll, shut it. You know nothin bout dat

They don't talk about the other kinds of junkies

Sensation Junkies

I-need-to-do-it-to say-i-did-it-kinda-junkies, Passion Junkies

They all look the same like the kinds of ones who jones so hard for a fix that no pipe, no crack, nothing that could, would taut-tighten-up the cheeks harder as they drag it in with lips like they mean it.

They don't talk about the way they…the way we keep…

Q. Hold? Girl, what I really ask is when do you break that dam? When do you release…

A. You can't drag the long dragged, I've been to where heat never ends.

A Reverse Catechism of How to Take Yourself Back When the World is Demanding to Eat More Pieces of You

1. Unsocket, unseat your eyes, see the face that the world will not, won't, isn't allowed to. 2. Taste yourself upon your own tongue. Do you know your own flavors? 3. That building… the space wants your body. 4. Those people, they demand your bodyREFUSE THEM YOUR BODY (and you know what they say…don't give breathe to that smile, if you can, take your teeth with you, if you can…your whole spirit…DENY THEM). 5. If you find yourself in that place or that place with them, with your own bound feet, wrists, and hooded head…kidnap yourself from their laps with necessary violence. 6. Be the disappeared on your own terms: they don't need to know. 7. Remain disappeared…you owe them nothing. 8. Block your ears from the noise…what she say, he say, they say in passing…as help as advice with tone, all mood, all will with no fucks for you…careful. The noise here will deaf and death you. 9. With full audacity as your birth right because you never apologized for the way you wailed unapologetic when your only language was primal. Sonic. The very first lullaby you heard and forgot because of all of the noise. 10. Go back to the before…

Before there was anything you were ever assigned -
do you remember what it was to be infinity?

Before being dipped in skin inheritance?

Before you knew you were anything separate?
Before you saw your own face to when you just were?

Before you were imprinted with a name, maybe you were in the garden
that time that Eve had wisdom to take away such prisons…

Before you were ever standing, walking, running, sitting…back to when you never needed nor asked for any kind of permission to float because time never worked like that there?

We tricked you, those statements posing as questions….you aren't ever given that kinda warning

And this is why I must tell you. It is written in an ink and alphabet you can't read. In fact I don't need to tell you. You don't need to hear it from the sound of my voice.

Stop listening.
You already know how to do it….you had it before you came here.

Dark Things We Don't Know Much About: Epilogue

What the jars are really used for
(buttons, bones, and the other things and   other things)
bridges and roads, all unnatural things
that told us about getting to the other side
(We were never spose'd to see what the self-induced
schizophrenia really is. Splitting self into shadow into…)
Now, it follows me, I can't tell the difference
How does a begotten thing of a begotten thing of a begotten
thing all unknown things, know that?

Dark things in daylight at first friendly
The reflection, how its us 1000 years from now,
Transfixed by the awe and beauty of the collision
The dirt, how its calm instructs on getting to a place
Raised against night's yawn   turn around if you've
never seen it in daylight   The voice comes out of
nowhere   it's in your face, it calls your name
Were you looking too hard? Don't listen to that message

Right now, it's too late. In walking, in conversation with yourself
you don't want what else is listening to get any notions
Get the jars, the ones that   and   from
Get the other one   (You don't know shit but   you do know shit)
Remember, we told you how to do it

The Reflection

This part

Hello hello Goodbye like yes no

yes

the transfallacy *yes,* it lies to you and to everyone
perhaps you need to perceive that which is deeper than you
knnnnoooooowwwww

for I shall dig as the Goonphucker sows and reaps what you know
cryptocryo frozen gold
lithium, silver hmmmm and mold
as in decay in society's way I laugh at you
I've been here since the dawn of day

Watching you with a singular eye, I've not yet given up my armor
For I'm an angel, I still fly

[Goonphucker laughs]

That's all I'll say

Notes

Blame No One But (I) and Blame No One But (II)

Both ekphrastic pieces are connected to the Lawson family murder in which Charles Davis Lawson murdered his family, then himself in 1929. Both pieces were inspired by the final family photo.

Sisters of She of Feral Souls, She Thangs, and…

This piece has been inspired by many things. My love for the intersection of horror and religion (so, many movies over time), in addition to real life scandals involving convents. Historical inspirations have included and are not limited to: Magdaline laundries of Ireland, the nuns of Sant'Ambrogio, and Mother Mariam Soulakiotis.

Confessions of the Last Pleasure Benefactrix for the Dead: The Last Pleasure Eater

Given some of the ancient practices of sin eaters and other traditions (like individuals sitting with the recently deceased), I was inspired to think about this question: what if there were eaters of pleasure, not sin, as a part of the final rites? What would that look like? What would this experience feel like?

Does the Body Dream Itself Into the Maze It Can't Escape?

This piece is sectioned using the Cistercian numeral system. It is intended to allow any number from 1 to 9999 to be conveyed as a symbol. The piece also includes a small piece of the song lyric from the 1987 song, "Fishnet," by Morris Day.

Suicide By Proxy: ~~Suicide by~~ Sacrifice

This was inspired by two sources. The film, *The Devils Bath* (2024) directed by Severin Fiala, Veronika Franz. The directors of the film came across the work of historian Kathy Stuart who wrote, *Suicide by Proxy in Early Modern Germany: Crime, Sin and Salvation*. The book covers the subject matter of "suicide by proxy," in which individuals would commit crimes in order to be punished to execution. These individuals committed crimes that allowed them to circumvent the church (given that suicide was a sin that would damn the soul to hell). This subject inspired the film and both sources inspired some of the material within the poem.

The other part of the long poem is inspired by what is referred to as a legend connected to the Crow Tribe. In Billings, Montana, there was a tragedy that has different variations that end with a couple of the Crow members sacrificing their lives by blinding their horses and riding them off of the cliff in order to join the family they lost during the tragedy. There are various sources, including some articles within the *Billings Gazette* that share parts of the tale.

Goonphucker's Last Riddle

The concept of the pre/trans – phallacy is a term used by Ken Wilber in the *Theory of Everything* and within much of his work. It points to the ways that our thinking and answers as a collective, while appearing the same on the surface, really contain levels of nuance depending on our consciousness.

Acknowledgements

The following poems have appeared in other publications and may have been slightly edited in the preparation of this current work.

This list of poems appeared in the chapbook, *This Is How They Teach You How to Want It...The Slaughter: A Field Guide for the Hunted & the Hunter, The Dead-Alive, The Live-Dead Ones, The...*: (Harbor Editions, 2024)

The Corpsed Eater
The Fevered Feral Suite
This Story Is About
Hallowed Haunted Body
The short preface to the Fevered Feral suite (on p. 21) originally appeared to be spoken by an entity know as The Bricklayer in the chapbook referenced.
You know the dead

Items that appeared in other publications:

Fevered Dreams of a Feral (I) appeared in the literary magazine, ITERANT (Issue #8), Iterant.org

Hallowed Haunted Body appeared in *Sign & Breath:Voice and the Literary Tradition* (Etruscan Press, 2025) that I co-edited with Philip Brady

"A Reverse Catechism of How to Take Yourself Back When the World is Demanding to Eat More Pieces of You," *Lily Poetry Review*, Jan–Feb. 2026.

"Catechistic Danger," "You Know the Dead," and "The Gloomslinger's Riddle," *Ploughshares,* Spring 2026.

About the Author

Shanta Lee Honeycutt is an award-winning visual artist, writer across genres, author, independent curator, and scholar who often says she is a "…practitioner of entanglement" for the ways she creates dialogue across mediums within her work. Her awards include the New England Poetry Club's Grant for Poetic Achievement, Abel Meeropol Social Justice Writing Award, a 2024 - 25 National Arts Strategies Creative Community Fellow (New England), the Arthur Williams Award for Meritorious Service to the Arts and in 2020, and New England Newspaper & Press Association (NENPA) awards for her journalism. Shanta Lee's work has been widely featured in *Ploughshares, The Poetry Foundation, Harper's Magazine, The Massachusetts Review, ITERANT Literary Magazine, Palette Poetry, CARVE Magazine, Ms. Magazine, DAME Magazine*, the *CounterText: A Journal for the Study of the Post-Literary* in the UK, and elsewhere.

Shanta Lee's previous books include: Co-Editor with Philip Brady of the anthology, *Sign & Breath: Voice and the Literary Tradition* (Etruscan Press, 2025); A double volume of two chapbooks, *Close Is... and Hopscotch Between the Living and the Dead* (Diode Editions, 2024); *This Is How They Teach You How to Want It...The Slaughter: A Field Guide for the Hunted & the Hunter, The Dead-Alive, The Live-Dead Ones, The...* (Harbor Editions, 2024); *Black Metamorphoses*—named a finalist in the 2021 Hudson Prize, shortlisted for the 2021 Cowles Poetry Book Prize and longlisted for the 2021 Idaho Poetry Prize—illustrated by Alan Blackwell (Etruscan Press, 2023); and *GHETTOCLAUSTROPHOBIA: Dreamin of Mama While Trying to Speak Woman in Woke Tongues* (Diode Editions, 2021), winner of the Vermont Book Award. Shanta Lee's photography has been featured in exhibitions and published in a few places. Her current and ongoing multi-medium series is *Dark Goddess.*

Shanta Lee also has a broad professional wingspan with successes that have included everything from the creation and implementation of 3 programs that continued for many years after her tenure, the creation of an artist salon, and co-creating "CreateVT," the creative sector's strategic plan for the state of Vermont. She has an MFA in Creative Non-Fiction and Poetry at the Vermont College of Fine Arts, an MBA from the University of Hartford, and an undergraduate degree in Women, Gender and Sexuality from Trinity College. Shanta Lee is a sucker for all things horror and true crime in addition to any adventure that might bring her face-to-face with a ruin or abandoned space.

Explore her work by visiting, Shantalee.com.

About Small Harbor Publishing

Small Harbor Publishing is a 501c3 nonprofit organization. Our goal is to publish unique and diverse voices. We are a feminist press, and we are committed to diversity and inclusion. We strive to bring new voices to a devoted and expanding readership.

Small Harbor Publishing began in 2018 with the first issue of *Harbor Review*. The magazine is an online space where poetry and art converse. *Harbor Review* quickly grew and now publishes reviews and runs multiple micro chapbook competitions, including the Washburn Prize and the Editor's Prize.

In July 2020, Small Harbor Publishing was officially incorporated and began Harbor Editions. Harbor Editions accepts submissions through a chapbook open reading period, a hybrid chapbook open reading period, the Marginalia Series, and the Laureate Prize.

In 2023, Harbor Anthologies began with a mission to promote texts that explore social justice issues and highlight marginalized writers.

If you would like to support Small Harbor Publishing, visit our "About" page at: smallharborpublishing.com/about.

www.ingramcontent.com/pod-product-compliance
Lightning Source LLC
LaVergne TN
LVHW091144080826
845145LV00008B/2245

* 9 7 8 1 9 5 7 2 4 8 6 5 3 *